COOPERATION COUNTS!

Life-Saving Strategies
For Parenting Toddlers to Teens

JEAN HAMBURG, LICSW

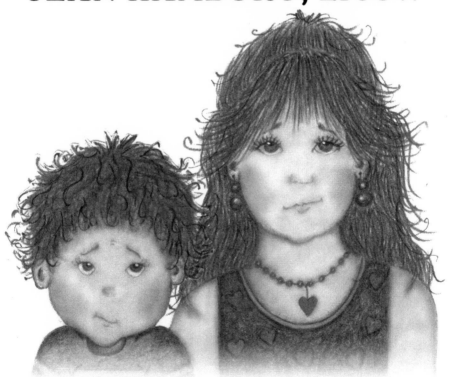

Illustrated by Barb English

Outskirts Press, Inc.
Denver, Colorado

Dedication

For my parents, Morey and Ruth, and for my Uncle Dave.
I miss them dearly.

Acknowledgments

I would like to applaud those parents who continue to search for ways to enjoy healthier family relationships. You are my inspiration and have my highest respect.

I am so very grateful to my family, who constantly show me how to share kindness, joy, and peaceful problem-solving in so many ways, every day, and not just during the easy times. Jackie, Julie and Laura, Aunt Betty, Greg and Dee Dee, Jeff and Lilli Ann, Sue and Mark, Alison and all the kids, thank you, everybody!

Thanks go to my multi-talented, much loved Godchildren, Joanna and Daniel along with their amazing parents, Debra and Chad, who constantly impress me with their humor, love of learning and enjoyment of each day. I am honored to be a part of your family!

It has been wonderful to be able to spend so many pleasant hours with Barb, my delightful cousin and illustrator extraordinaire, exploring the intricacies of human nature via the faces of the Cooperation Counts kids. Your endless patience has been truly amazing. Thank you, Barb!

Kudos to my consultants. Thank you, Katherine Reeder, LMHC, Rahmi Hartati, Ed.M, Janet Smedile, B.S., and Kathleen Smith, co-copyeditor!

And then there is my step-mother Marian, who is my cheer-leader, who firmly believes that sharing the Cooperation Counts program with families is the right thing to do, and has enthusiastically insisted that I "Get going and do it!" Thank you, Mom!

I have saved this special place to acknowledge Davida Rosenblum, my editor, who, as it turns out, has been my caring advisor through many moments of joy as well as tribulation. She, too, has cared deeply that the Cooperation Counts program be shared. Magically, she knew what kind of support I needed and when I needed it, by sharing her wisdom, talent, humor, "talkings-to" and everything in between. Thank you, Davida!

Table of Contents

THE PUZZLING WORLD OF PARENTING

I can't remember what it was that pushed me over the top one hot summer day in the year 2003, but it was clearly child related, and my mood was definitely not serene.

Here I was, a seasoned psychotherapist and mother of two internationally adopted daughters. In both my personal and professional lives I was familiar with many wonderful parenting programs. Even so, I was just about ready to throw in the proverbial towel.

Shower Power

Enough was enough! The only place I could think, where I would not be disturbed, was the shower. So I decided to get into it and not come out until I had figured out even the beginning of an answer to the question, "Why won't the kids just behave?" Thankfully, I came up with an insight pretty quickly: It was because they *just don't want to*!

I had been trying to force my kids to cooperate in every conniving and convincing way I knew how, and we were all exhausted and exasperated. When I realized that the key was in finding a way to help my kids to WANT to cooperate, I knew I would have a much easier time.

What emerged then, over time, was the Cooperation Counts program, which I have introduced to countless families with amazing results. Encouraged by the recommendations of these much happier families, I decided to put the tools of the program into book form.

I hope that other stressed and exhausted families may benefit from the following pages and find more joy, happiness and fun in their family lives together.

WHAT IS THE COOPERATION COUNTS SYSTEM AND WHY DOES IT WORK?

The Cooperation Counts system includes a series of time warnings, counting clues, 3's, work-off's and stars. All are designed to address complicated parenting dilemmas. The steps are deceptively simple, but don't underestimate their positive power.

Cooperation Counts is a combination of several of the most effective child management techniques designed to increase cooperation between adults and children. It is a simple system that addresses not-so-simple issues that include tantrums, refusals, sibling rivalry, won't do homework, getting-up grumpiness, bedtime blues, supermarket scenes, talking back, obnoxious attitudes, school situations, wailing and flailing, curfew concerns, refusing to put things away, and even running-everybody-ragged-with-demands difficulties. The program is designed to get through the tough times and bring out the best in everyone.

Discipline and Praise

Every family needs a reasonable framework for discipline and praise, but this is often easier said than done. Let's face it. Relationships are complicated under any and all circumstances. When the framework for navigating the tough (as well as the easy) times is in place, the real goal can then be achieved. This goal is for adults to look for, find, develop, and use additional parenting skills that encourage happier outcomes. These are skills which do not necessarily come naturally. It is quite a trick to be able to think clearly when one's blood is boiling. Using some simple strategies that help to deal with miserable moments can, in itself, be invaluable. The Cooperation Counts program offers strategies for parents who wish to cope with the tough times and move on toward the business of enjoying the kids and each other.

> *This simple method of behavior management gives parents concrete tools to address normal, usual, age appropriate difficulties as well as more intense, disruptive ones.*

The Problem:
Why There is a Need for This Book

To start the process of attempting to get what they want, kids of all ages know what they need to do. The techniques have been perfected. They include begging, whining, crying, teasing, refusing, screaming, or shutting down. They might even throw in some rolling around on the floor, and by that time the adults are often rendered helpless.

We start reasoning, arguing, refusing, raising our voices, threatening, calling for back-up, and a host of other desperate measures.

Within seconds, adults find themselves in the position of wondering what to do. Aren't kids amazing? Even very young children know how to get otherwise well-put-together adults into I-have-no-idea-what-to-do mode.

What is a Red Flag?
What is Just Kids' Stuff?

Even when our children are babies, we start to wonder about what is an age appropriate behavior and what is a red flag. Using the Cooperation Counts program helps to sort out the answers to these questions.

Mystery Moments

When life in the parenting department is rolling along smoothly, parenting can be a great deal of fun. But then there are the mystery moments.

Children can run out to play at 100 mph, but when it comes to moving it along in the mornings, turtle mode rules!

Kids and teens of all ages can sit quietly for hours in front of the TV, but when it comes to sitting quietly in the car for even five minutes, mayhem ensues!

In the store, the rule is to hold the adult's hand. Quicker than anyone can say "ice cream," the hand that was supposed to be connected is clearly not, and Johnny is racing down the canned vegetables isle heading for the toys. He will go to great lengths to avoid even the thought of being near a vegetable, but in this scene, whizzing by the hated items doesn't seem to create the slightest bit of stress!

This is the same child who just last night could not manage to head down the hall at a reasonable pace towards bed. Yes, that's him all right, the one running at the speed of light past the vegetables, in the illegal direction of the toys!

A Solution: Use the Cooperation Counts Program

This system has developed into an easy-to-use, daily life program that can be implemented by any family, regardless of history, diagnosis, or circumstances.

Dr. Thomas W. Phelan, author of the highly regarded book *1-2-3 Magic, Effective Discipline for Children 2-12, Fourth Edition* (Parent Magic, Inc., 2010) has graciously permitted the use of his counting clues method to be included in the beginning portion of the Cooperation Counts program, which is designed in such a way that adults are able to use one simple, respectful set of strategies to address multiple behaviors of concern for children ages 2-15.

With an effective framework for discipline and praise in place, additional parenting strategies can then be introduced in calm, conscious, more thoughtful ways.

Power struggles, yelling, whining, talking back and flat-out refusals seem to disappear as the adults step back from trying to force an outcome. Adults no longer need to be the "bad guy," even when it is consequence time.

Presenting the Program to the Kids

1 2 3

Presenting the program in an upbeat way is essential. Have some fun with it. Gather the family. Give the information clearly and concisely, without getting derailed onto any other subject.

Hold up a sign with a **1**, **2** and a **3**. You can find one on the website www.cooperationcounts.com or make your own. Then, say something like this:

"We've decided that we want to cut down on yelling and nagging, so we're going to use something called the Cooperation Counts system. That's where you get to decide if you want to cooperate with us or not.

Basically, choosing a 3 is not a happy choice for you. But earning stars is great. Any 3's you decide to get belong to us and will need to be worked off sometime when something is really important, like if someone invites you to go somewhere. The work-off might be that you will need to wait a while to go, or even that it might not happen at all. Your job will be to decide whether or not to get 3's. Our job, sadly, will be to get them worked off. The good news is that once 3's are worked off, they are done! That's it!

As for the stars, they're given for deciding to make good choices. Ten stars equal something special. We're going to watch for star choices and cheer you on to get them!

You will each have a 3's chart and a stars chart. When we ask you to cooperate with something, we'll give you time warnings and then counting clues, so that you can think about what you want your choice to be.

Any behavior that is violent or hurts someone is an automatic 3.

"That's 1" is OK but it means we're serious, and now it's up to you to decide whether or not to cooperate.

"That's 2" is OK but it's only three seconds away from the 3.

If you decide to cooperate by 1 or by 2, that's great. You have decided to avoid the sad 3.

"That's 3" is not OK because it will need to be worked off sometime when something is important to you.

We will decide, in a calm way, what the work-off will be and when it will happen.

Good luck with your choices!"

Jimmy

Six-year-old Jimmy refuses to stay in his own bed, coming in to his parents at various times during the night, waking both parents and causing a scene. Everyone is exhausted from lack of sleep, from arguing, convincing, yelling, punishing, bribing, or ignoring. Cooperation Counts is presented and the following week we hear that Jimmy has been sleeping in his own room and has been tip-toeing to the bathroom and back without disturbing either parent. His parents are rested, and little Jimmy is proud of his recent choices.

Adults learn tools for being clear and respectful when making requests, not falling into the usual traps of tantrums, blaming, arguments, and other power struggles. They learn to follow through with meaningful and manageable consequences, implemented calmly and with genuine empathy. When children are given chances to make choices, they tend not to need to be as defensive or oppositional. Boundaries can be put into place without power struggles, even if the child's choice is a decision *not* to cooperate.

Billy, Betty, Bobby and Barbara

Billy, Betty, Bobby and Barbara (ages four to eleven) fight constantly at home and in stores. Whenever they visit their friends' homes, however, they are suddenly model children. Their parents are beside themselves with frustration and have no idea what else they could possibly do. Their marriage is showing

signs of strain. The Cooperation Counts system is put into place and the fighting stops.

Although adults usually ask children to cooperate in ordinary areas of daily life, they often choose not to, leaving adults unsure about what to do. The usual interventions of reasoning, explaining, bribing, threatening, punishing, or yelling often have little impact and usually lead to conflicts, anger, and more refusals. Cooperation Counts has helped many children and adults to get "unstuck," with everyone accepting the process as well as the outcome.

Suzy

Three-year-old Suzy has been intentionally urinating and defecating on the floor, refusing to use the toilet in direct and open defiance of all requests, although she has been fully potty trained. Cooperation Counts is put into place, and the very same day she voluntarily uses the bathroom. Months later, there are still no difficulties.

Minnie

Thirteen-year-old Minnie is rude, refuses to help around the house, and is doing poorly in school. She tells everyone that she hates herself and can't stand her parents and teachers. She has several good friends and many supports, but she continues to underachieve at school and make life miserable at home.

The Cooperation Counts system is introduced, and within a few weeks, she decides to talk in respectful tones, gets after-school help and has even been seen laughing with her parents.

These stories all demonstrate what happens when families have the courage to try new parenting approaches.

If you think of parenting as an incredibly complex project and look only at the big picture, it can be mind-boggling. But breaking down an overwhelming task has definite advantages.

Simplifying

For example, in computer land, at least some of us may spend an inordinate amount of time figuring out how to send a large file without crashing the recipient's system. But actually, there is an easy, quick way to do that. Using the program tools can get complicated parenting "files" organized in a flash.

The Cooperation Counts program does not just list the troubles; it gives tools to deal with them so that positive parenting replaces impulsive parenting.

About the Tricky Business of Parenting Teens

The Cooperation Counts program applies just as clearly when parenting teens. By using the program scripts and steps you are making needed changes for yourselves. This helps to avoid taking negatives personally while insisting on enjoying your teens whenever there is a window of opportunity to do so. More to the point, using the program gives you the strength to look for those windows.

Families who had given up hope and children who had shown great defiance are consistently regaining their ability to have fun together and live happier, more peaceful lives through the simple and easily implemented tools of Cooperation Counts.

FREQUENTLY ASKED QUESTIONS

How many steps must we learn?
Only a few. Old and young can learn the system in a very short time.

When can we start?
As soon as the adults decide to begin.

What if not all of the adults agree about using the Cooperation Counts system?
No problem. One parent can use it even if the other adults involved decide not to.

I have four kids of different ages. How can one program help us?
The program can be used for children of all ages as well as for families of all sizes and situations.

How long will it take to see an effect?
Anywhere from a few minutes to a few days. It all depends on how willing the adults are to stick with it, and it's not that hard.

What if my child has been acting up for a long time?
This is a very usual concern. It has no bearing on the use of the system or on the outcome. The strategies work equally well for casual as well as chronic misbehavior.

How hard is this to do?
Everything you and your child are asked to do can be accom-

plished. The adult's job is to commit to using the process, and the child's job is to realize that the behavior choice is theirs. And remember: Any child can cooperate with ordinary requests, *if she wants to.*

What if the adults are having trouble with their own anger toward the children?

Cooperation Counts provides effective tools to deal with issues in a non-emotional way, whether the children decide to cooperate or not. The program provides anger management for the adults as well as for the kids.

My child has a diagnosis and just can't help himself. What then?

I encourage the adults to remember to use the tools of the system, no matter what diagnosis there might be. Of course, adult requests need to be reasonable and possible for each particular child. Parents are responsible for obtaining diagnosis and treatment information for their children's specific needs. Encouraging all children to try their best is a very good thing. And remember that all-important difference between "I can't" and "I won't!"

What if a child reacts with increased anger in response to the system?

No problem. This is a sign that you are getting the child's attention, and it will not interfere with the desired result. Using the tools of the system leaves previously helpless, worried, and overwhelmed adults with a plan that is fair and easily put into place. The kids can be empowered as well, since they have clear opportunities to make choices. Power struggles, the age-old bug-a-boo of every parent, becomes a thing of the past.

Will it disrupt my usual routine?
It's easy to integrate the system into everyday life. You will need only two pieces of paper, twelve seconds, and a little imagination.

Cooperation Counts Helps the Adults To:

- Establish a consistent framework for discipline and praise with follow-through for both.

- Give praise with enthusiasm.

- Let go of lectures.

- Get the children's attention.

- Say goodbye to grudges.

- Have conversations, not arguments.

- Disengage from negative scenes.

- Give information without nagging.

- Remember that no one enjoys being ordered to do something.

- Banish "because I said so!"

- Use consequences to replace punishments.

- Conserve much-needed adult energy.

- Develop and keep a good sense of humor.

What do Parenting and Trampolines Have in Common?

The system itself is simple but effective. The real value, however, comes from what happens after it is in place. Sitting or standing on a trampoline is not particularly impressive. Once you begin to bounce, that's a different story! All families need a plan for discipline and praise that provides the framework for daily life together. The bed of the trampoline is like that framework. Jumping is the vital part of finding and using thoughtful, effective parenting strategies.

When a Child Wants to Do Something and When a Child Does Not

You can put a child on a potty, but it is impossible to make her poop or pee into it.

You can insist that food go into a child's mouth, but it is impossible to make her chew and swallow it.

You can find ways to keep a child in a room when it is bedtime, but it is impossible to make her go to sleep.

What is missing from these impossible situations is one powerful word: *WANT*. If a child *wants* to pee and poop in a potty, *wants* to chew and swallow something–even a nasty something—and *wants* to let herself drift off to sleep, these situations change from the impossible to the very possible.

The word "want" is an important one indeed.

Can't vs. Won't; Shifting Parenting Gears

Kids and teens of all ages often try to convince adults that they just "can't" follow this or that request. It is definitely a very good thing for adults to be sure about the differences between "can't" and "won't."

Has a Child Ever Suffered Permanent Damage From Not Having French Fries?

There might be a case somewhere in the world, but I am not aware of it.

Expectations and Elephants:
Mission Impossible?

Have you ever asked your (any age) child—even a really smart one—to bring you the architectural designs of the Empire State Building, perfectly done in ten minutes, when your child doesn't even know what the words "architectural designs" mean? This is definitely an impossible expectation!

Have you ever asked your (any age) child—even a really brave one—to go out in the middle of the night alone in a howling snowstorm to the nearest CVS parking lot to find an elephant? I don't mean a baby elephant. I mean the adult-size one. Then have you told her to bring the elephant back to the house, squeeze it through the door, hold onto it for three hours…. and tell the elephant not…..to…..poop? Now, that would be impossible, and a bit harder, I suspect, than expecting your child to do things like: "Please put on your clothes"; "Please take off your clothes"; "Stop hitting your sister"; "Turn off the TV"; "Come in for dinner."

Let's make it perfectly clear that although sometimes kids will try to convince adults that they just *can't* do something, in reality, more likely they just *won't*.

About Elbows, Eyeballs, and Other Body Parts

In my therapy sessions, I always ask the children "Who is in charge of your eyeballs?" "I am" is always the answer. "Who is in charge of your arms, legs, toes, mouth, brain, your whole body?" "I am" is always the answer. Parents, fasten your symbolic seat belts, as it is often a shock to realize that we adults are not in charge of our children's bodies. They are.

Traps: Pitfalls for the Parents

Traps include the multiple ways that children try to avoid cooperating by taking the spotlight off the real issue. Kids are masterful at figuring out how to get this deed done. I often wonder at the level of their creativity in this area. Even pre-verbal kids can be characterized as masterful. Adults beware. Falling into a trap quickly becomes a slide down a slippery slope. Although the list of traps is endless here are a few typical ones:

> "You can't make me!"
> "I can't!"
> "I forgot!"
> "I don't care!"
> "Whatever..."
> "I hate you!"
> "You're so mean!"
> "I'm not doing anything you say!"

Screaming, arguing, slamming doors, giving horrible looks and rudeness.

Add to all of the above, and much more, IN PUBLIC!

Reasonable Responses

If you decide to respond to such traps at all, consider using only safe phrases such as "Thank you for letting me know." That's it. Anything more, I suggest, has the potential of heading towards that challenging slope—straight down—and frankly, one big goal of the program is to avoid these no-win scenes in the first place.

Power Struggles: Avoid Them Like the Plague

Power struggles are nasty business and adults will almost never win them. "I won't. You can't make me!" is a very true statement. Avoiding power struggles in every parent-child relationship is essential. The trick has been how to get that accomplished.

Using the tools of the Cooperation Counts program gets the job done without sapping much-needed energy from the adults. Following the system quickly helps to sort out what is a red flag one day from a situation that may fade from memory or interest the next.

What to do With Ever-Escalating Emotions

Replacing yelling, frustration, and lectures with the tools of the program provides an anger management plan for everyone.

Just as every flower needs a root system to hold it in place and to provide nutrients for it to flourish, so it is that for all families, a consistent system that can be depended upon must be in place to grow healthy relationships. Just as there is a delicate balance in nature, so it is in family life. Riding out the storms can be challenging, but satisfying as well.

When adults experience minimized anger, less frustration, lowered stress levels, less guilt—and can extricate themselves from the "because I said so" attitude—they are then in a position to think. Thinking can lead to making conscious choices to use positive parenting strategies that make sense.

> *The future is important and so is the past, but it is today that we can do something about. Each day is a gift, and there are always possibilities for change. Finding ways to have fun with each other counts for yesterday, today, and for tomorrow.*

CHAPTER 1
BASIC STEPS: COUNTING CLUES

The Script:
Give a time warning:
"In one minute it will be time to ....."
"It's almost time to...."
"Now it's time to...."

Wait for three seconds, saying nothing else.
"That's 1. Time to...." *and give counting clues as described below. If your child or teen decides to cooperate by 1 or 2, great! If not, say only,* **"That's 3."**

What Replaces What? The Interpretation of the Counting Clues

TIME WARNINGS: Replace **Nagging.**

ALMOST TIME... and NOW IT'S TIME: Replace **Begging.**

THAT'S ONE: The adult is serious. Replaces **Lectures.**

THAT'S TWO: The ball is in the child or teen's court to decide whether or not to cooperate. Replaces **Explaining.** Two is fine, but it is only three seconds away from 3.

THAT'S THREE: Means that's it. The decision has been made—and that's all it means. This replaces **Threats.**

AUTOMATIC 3: Anything that is risky, dangerous, or violent. This replaces **Adult Raging.**

About Yelling and Counting Clues

Every parent knows that yelling is ineffective. I believe that most of us do a fair amount of it because of a lot of factors, but one of them, at least in the parenting department, is because we are frustrated. We are frustrated because the kids are not cooperating, even though we know they could. Replacing yelling with time warnings and counting clues is a healthier alternative for everyone.

What Happens to 3's?

If the kids choose not to cooperate by the count of 3 that 3 is recorded on a chart. This is referred to as the kids "deciding to get a 3." Those 3's then belong to the adults and must be worked off (Chapter 2). A work-off is a consequence; it is not a punishment, but it is meaningful. The focus of the poor choice is not on the adult who is in an empathetic, supportive role when it is consequence time. Children's choices to decide to cooperate by one or by two are greeted with praise and joy.

The System: Give Time Warnings Followed by Counting Clues

This is not rocket science, but do not underestimate its importance. Preparing your child for a change (even an unwelcome change) at least sets the stage for the *possibility* of a willingness to comply. Having the information is better than a surprise. Start this way:

"In two minutes, it will be time to brush your teeth." Say nothing more.

When I recommend saying nothing more, I mean *SAY NOTHING MORE*—unless, of course, there is a conversation, not an argument. This might even be the time to commiserate about the inconvenience and dislike of the brushing of teeth; however, if the conversation shows any sign of turning into an argument, *STOP* and continue the time warnings:

"In one minute it will be time to brush your teeth." No matter what the kids say or do, it is not worth it to be lured off subject or into an argument.

"Now it's time to brush your teeth." Let's not worry about the outcome. Maybe the teeth will get brushed, maybe they won't.

As soon as you say, **"Now it's time….."** no more talk is needed. That means *NO* more talk because ***NOW IT IS TIME!***

If your child decides to cooperate, great! **"Thank You."**

25

If not, say only **"That's 1. Teeth please."** No more words are needed. Speak in a natural, firm tone. No theatrics. Four words. Terrific!

Wait for three seconds, saying nothing, then repeat the request. **"That's 2. Brush, please."** That's still only four words! You might even drop the "please," as the tone of voice should be a respectful, informational one.

About Waiting Until 2

Any choice to cooperate by one or by two is fantastic. Lots of kids will wait until two. No problem.

If you observe no teeth brushing going on, wait for another three seconds and say *only "***That's three.****"* No more discussion is needed except for giving one more set of counting clues—this time, minus the initial time warnings. No additional discussion. *This is vital.*

If brushing teeth has been picked as a "target behavior" and you would be tickled pink if there were to be cooperation in this area, the tooth brusher might be in line for an all-important star (Chapter 3).

NOTE: Counting clues are *never* to be drawn out, as in "That's one.......That's two.......That's two and a half....."

The All-Important 3's Chart

3's

name: _____

	PROBLEM	WORK OFF
date____ ▯	_____	_____
date____ ▯	_____	_____
date____ ▯	_____	_____
date____ ▯	_____	_____
date____ ▯	_____	_____
date____ ▯	_____	_____
date____ ▯	_____	_____
date____ ▯	_____	_____

Charts and other materials are available via the website www.cooperationcounts.com or families are welcome to make their own.

Write the 3 in the box on the chart. Date it. No discussion at this time. Resist the urge to lecture, shout, cry, beg, bribe, or swear. On the "Problem" line, write "no teeth brushing." The work-off line will be left for the consequence, which is not written on the chart until the work-off is done.

When you delay or forget to put the 3's up promptly and clearly, then the system is compromised, paving the way for the old power struggles and poor choices. Even if that happens, getting back to Cooperation Counts basics is always better than yelling, sarcasm, or complaining. Adults decide when they start to count, and if they do, the kids know it is now *up to them* to decide. So, take heart. Go with the system as written. Accept any 3's the kids decide to get, while remaining calm, even if your emotions say the opposite.

What Happens at "That's 3?"

Any 3's the kids decide to get belong to the adults and must be worked off (Chapter 2). Each child or teen will have a visible accounting of her 3's. This can be on a chart, sticky note, napkin, piece of Kleenex, or a used scrap of paper. 3's have even been recorded on adult hands as well as on phones and laptops (Chapter 8). Cooperation Counts is definitely a portable daily life-friendly system.

Children have choices whether or not to cooperate with usual (even if unpopular) requests. Parents are able to move out of the bad-guy/punisher role.

We have heard counting clues being given in all sorts of settings and in all sorts of tones of voices. But there is no mystery about what they mean when the Cooperation Counts program is in place.

Interpretation of Counting Clues: Cooperation Counts Style

The meaning of each counting clue can be learned quickly and easily, even by very young children. ONE means that the adult is serious and it is now up to the kids about whether or not they will decide to cooperate. TWO is o.k. but is only three seconds away from the sad 3. Any 3's the kids decide to get, belong to the adults and will need to be worked off (Chapter 2).

Reminder About Automatic 3's:

If a behavior is risky or violent, it is not advised to give time warnings or counting clues. Most families identify this category to include behaviors such as kicking, pinching, biting, scratching, or hurting in any way. What is and is not an automatic 3 is left to the discretion of the adults.

SCOTT AND THE PEAR

It was Christmas time and the tree was up, but Scott, age five, often decided not to cooperate with the family rules. His brothers and sister were not happy about this situation, mostly because their parents often got angry. A lot of the anger had to do with the fact that even the most patient of the crew usually ended up being exasperated with Scott.

Both parents and all four kids agreed: Nothing was really important to Scott. Working with the Cooperation Counts system was hitting a dead end, because, they said, absolutely no consequences fit into the category of "important" to Scott.

One day, while I was having a meeting with his parents, Scott wandered into the living room and asked for a pear. His Mom asked him to wait until our meeting was over, but he would have none of that. Scott whined and begged for the pear. He was told the same thing. His response was the same, and I could see the frustration settling over his parents, just as they had been reporting all along.

I suggested using the Cooperation Counts program tools. We were soon to start with work-offs of 3's (Chapter 2) but for right now, it was just **"That's 3. Time-out"**—the ten second variety.

Scott asked (actually begged) for the pear yet again. The pear certainly seemed important to Scott!

Using the Counting Clues to Get Scott's Attention

Mom: **"In one minute, it will be time to stop asking about the pear."**

Mom: **"It's almost time to stop asking about the pear."**

Mom: **"Now it's time to stop talking about the pear."** (Key words: **"Now it's time…"**).

Scott: "I want the pear."

Mom: **"That's one. No more pear talk."**

Scott: "I want the pear."

Mom: **"Scott, that's two. No more pear talk."**

Scott: "I want the pear *NOW!*"

Mom: **"That's 3. Time-out!"**

Using the Counting Clues to Remove Adult Attention

Mom took Scott to his room (without saying one word, removing all attention), closed the door, waited five seconds, then asked, in an upbeat tone of voice, if he was all done with his time-out. She asked if he was all set for no more pear talk. Scott nodded. He got a big hug. Down he came, and as he did so, he very purposefully touched the Christmas tree—a huge no-no. One 3 had already been put on his chart: "Pear talk." Another 3 had now been put on his chart: "Touching the tree."

Getting Scott's Attention Again

He had another short time-out and was back in the living room again promptly. We had his attention. He had wanted the pear. It was clear that he had been intentionally "messing" with us. But by using the system, his parents were clear, respectful, and not engaged in any arguing.

"The work-off of these two 3's...pear talk and touching the tree...is to wait for five minutes to have the pear and the time starts when you are nice and settled down!"

We set the timer for five minutes and when it went off, that would be the time to have his pear. We wanted to keep his attention and set him up for success. Then, we would see what he would decide. Key words: *HE WOULD DECIDE.*

The timer was set. Scott went over to the tree and decided to touch it again.

"Oh, no!" we all said in chorus mode. **"The time needs to start all over again."**

The timer was re-set (no other talk from the adults). Things went along great. Scott was looking at a book—quietly—with the timer in front of him. We praised him.

Then, it happened.

Scott said, "I want a pear."

"Oh no!" went the chorus… and the timer was re-set. There was quiet from Scott. We went on with our conversation, but each of us cheered him on by saying from time to time, **"Yay! Only two more minutes to go!"**

More countdown. Quiet from Scott. No tree was touched. No pear was requested. We were smiling at him and then the timer went off. We all clapped and cheered. Scott smiled from ear to ear. Mom went to get the pear and Scott ate it. Happiness for Scott was eating a legal pear!

As soon as the pear disappeared, Scott wanted a banana. Before Mom could say yes or no, he ran over to the timer and asked Dad to set it!

Scott waited. No tree was touched; the banana lay on the coffee table until it was OK to eat it. We clapped and cheered again, thanked Scott for his wonderful waiting, and he enjoyed his banana. Anger had been replaced with smiles, which always trump frowns. The scene that we enjoyed most was when Scott *wanted the timer set* to let him know when he could have the banana. Limits requested by his parents were accepted as his *own* choice. The transfer of power, done peacefully, was successfully in place. His family could enjoy him more and he could enjoy his banana!

Common Household Hazards

Adults talk too much. Kids talk too much.

Adults argue too much. Kids argue too much.

Use Very Few Words

Lose the lectures. The kids are not interested, and you get exhausted. Play a game with yourself. Use as few words as possible. Count the number of words used and congratulate yourself on

any lower number. For example, *DON'T* say, "It is really important that your teeth are brushed before you go to bed because if
you don't, bacteria will grow on them and you will end up with
cavities and I will end up with a big dental bill. Now, I know
you don't want that to happen so it is really important for you to
get that brushing going."

See what I mean? I will bet money that after the first few words,
any hint of interest is rapidly replaced with thinking about other
important things, which most likely do not have anything even
remotely to do with teeth!

No Threats, Please

Ban "If you don't watch out, you're going to get a 3." Threats are
not a part of the program.

Refuse to March into Battle

Ugly power struggles are avoided just by using the Cooperation
Counts program steps. Refusing to fight is a handy tool to
have.

Never Say: "You HAVE To ..."

Since kids are in charge of themselves, they actually don't *have*
to do anything they don't want to do. If parents say, "You HAVE

to...." they are left in the unenviable position of looking foolish when a child just won't. It is difficult to preserve any semblance of dignity in those circumstances, so I suggest they be avoided altogether.

Making a Request Cooperation Counts Style

Go over to your child. Be close enough so that you know she can hear your words. Avoid power struggles by *NOT*, for example, asking her to come to you, telling her to look into your eyes or to repeat what you have said, because maybe she will and maybe she won't.

Anger Management: Giving Counting Clues Allows Adults and Kids to Take a Breather

Emotions often run high when the children don't want to co-operate and for the adults who are often outraged at their lack of compliance. Time warnings, counting clues, 3's, work-offs (Chapter 2) and stars (Chapter 3) help everyone to step back from the often intense battle of wills.

Kids are Not Counters

Kids and teens will try to give counting clues to each other as well as to their parents. This is not an option. In addition, teasing by siblings or making light of "That's one" is counterproductive and should be discouraged and if the kids decide to keep going, you might decide to request that this stop and if it doesn't, begin the counting clues as described.

Any 3's the Kids Decide to Get Belong to the Adults and Will Need to be Worked Off

A work-off is a consequence, not a punishment. The way work-off's are done is vital to the system and details will be discussed in the next chapter.

Only Two Sets of Counting Clues Should Be Given

If the kids decide twice to get to three and not brush their teeth, this translates into the dreaded power struggle scene, which you will usually never win, so don't even try. *STOP GIVING COUNTING CLUES AFTER TWO ROUNDS.*

What Happens if the Teeth Don't Get Brushed?

Then they don't get brushed. Have you ever heard of a child who has actually needed to be hospitalized from not brushing his teeth for a night or two? There might be a case somewhere in the world, but frankly, I haven't heard of any. The teeth may not get brushed, but the 3 (or two 3's) will be on his chart.

Those 3's will belong to the adults, and will need to be worked off sometime when something is really important and when that something will or won't happen no matter what she says or does. Of course, if Miss-Usually-Does-Not-Brush-Her-Teeth were to decide to do so, that would be a wonderful choice and a star could be placed on her star chart (Chapter 3).

A Reminder About Automatic 3's

Whenever possible, it is always a good idea to give counting clues, since doing so puts the kids on notice to decide what to do. When a parent says a behavior is an automatic 3, it is an automatic 3. End of story.

When the "Three-Seconds-Between-the-Numbers Rule" Does Not Apply

Use parental judgment. For example, your child spits. One option is to ask him to stop. If he doesn't, another option is to give counting clues. If the spitter decides to stop doing so by one or by two and then, a minute or two later decides to spit again, **"That's 3. No spitting."** The 3 goes on the chart, belongs to the adults, and will need to be worked off. If the spitting continues, another set of counting clues can be given but after the second set, *STOP,* as it is now clear that this is a spitting power struggle. Even if the nasty behavior continues, there will at least be a plan in the form of a work-off at an appropriate time. Do not discuss it until it is time for the work-off. If the spitting continues, it is advised to remove the "audience" by paying no attention to this messy scene.

Nipping the Negatives in the Bud

A good time to consider giving counting clues is when you start to feel annoyed.

You decide when to start to count. So, take heart. Go with the system as written. Stick with respectful tones and use very few words. Accept any 3's the kids decide to get while remaining calm, even if your blood pressure is heading up!

MORNING MADNESS: PART I
COUNTING CLUES STYLE

Sandy (8), Molly (9), and Ken (11) were constantly late for their ride to school. Their parents finally decided they wanted to have a chance to avoid gray hair and blood pressure issues, and maintain some semblance of dignity by using the Cooperation Counts tools. If the kids decided to cooperate, great. If they decided not to, their parents gave them another set of counting clues. This is plenty of time to decide to get moving, or not. The parents wanted to save wear and tear on their energy reserve, which is a very good thing, considering that it was still early in the morning and there were many more hours of the day yet to go.

Time warnings were given to the group by Dad: **"In ten minutes, the car will be leaving."** He refrained from getting into the trap of reminding the kids of every little detail—over and over. Conversation is fine; nagging is not.

"In five minutes, the car will be leaving."

"In one minute the car will be leaving."

"It's almost time to leave."

"Now it's time to get into the car." He said nothing else except to proceed with the counting clues as described at the beginning of the chapter.

If anyone decided not to be in the car by three, the 3 would go on her chart(s), belong to the parents, and would be worked off at an appropriate time (Chapter 2). If Dad decided that two sets of counting clues would be given, then he would give them. He did not say anything other than giving the counting clues. Staying focused on the **"Now it's time to get into the car"** request was what was important, and that's what Dad did.

Without saying any more words, it was time to head the car out. Molly and Ken were in the car. Sandy was not. (If a child is too young to stay at home, she should be walked or carried to the car, without any talking by the adult. If a child is able to stay alone for a few minutes, the others could be dropped of at school until Dad returned to the house.)

Let's say it was ice cream day at school. Sandy decided to get two 3's in the turtle mode exit from the house. At drop off, she asked for her ice cream money. Dad checked to see if there were any 3's on her chart that needed to be worked off. On this day, he had actually attached a sticky note to the dashboard of the car, and his response to the ice cream money request was to say, **"Let's check your sticky note."** Then he read off, in an informational tone, **"I see two 3's: Not getting into the car on time this morning--twice."** Pause. Think. **"The work-off of these two 3's is no ice cream money today,"** said in a kindly, empathetic tone, of course. (Chapter 2)

Dad refused to put on the punisher hat. He used a calm tone of voice, avoided the phrase "You can't have ice cream money today," and he avoided any mention of Sandy's poor choice. He acted sad, for real.

Sandy's two 3's were simply entered on her chart at home on two of the "Problem" lines: "Late for ride to school" (twice).

"No ice cream money" was entered twice on the "Work-off" lines.

That was that. The 3's were worked off and everyone moved on with the day.

Later, Dad was on the look-out for a quiet moment to be with Sandy and offered: **"Would you like to think of some ways to figure out how to be in the car on time tomorrow morning?"**

If Sandy was not ready for such a conversation, that would be clear. Dad would drop it and move on. This would not be a time for lectures. If ideas were forthcoming, that would be wonderful, because when children are involved in their own problem-solving, they are often more motivated to follow through.

42

The next morning, yelling and nagging were once again replaced with time warnings and counting clues. No one knew what Sandy would decide to do about getting into the car on time, but she and her siblings would still be given chances to make their choices—respectfully, of course—and minus yelling, lectures, and nagging.

Keep in Mind

If the kids decide not to have breakfast due to dilly-dallying getting into the car, remember that lunch or a snack would most likely be available later on. Perhaps there might be some granola bars that live in the car. Even if there were to be a response such as "I hate granola bars," it would be very sad about the sparse car menu selection. Very sad.

But what if the kids decide to cooperate by one, two, or even just at a request? Stars will abound as a reward to reinforce their wonderful choice. (Chapter 3)

There Is a Plan if the Kids Decide to Cooperate, and There Is a Plan if They Don't

Any 3's kids decide to get will be charted. As we will see in the next chapter, there will be a *consequence* of choosing a 3—*not a punishment for having chosen it.*

Time Warnings and Counting Clues Replace Yelling

Using these tools is what helps you to remain C...A...L...M. There is great joy if the kids decide to cooperate, and there is a respectful plan if the kids decide not to.

A Word of Caution about Possible Responses to 3's

All children will decide to get some 3's. Responses vary widely, from resignation to rage. Although intense displays of emotion are not easy to see or hear, they are not a reason to give in. If parents give in, this is a sign to the kids that all they need to do is object loudly enough and they will get their original wish. This message creates havoc with any attempt to keep some sort of order in parent/child relationships. Using the program steps addresses this challenging area directly, respectfully, and swiftly. The goal of moving on through the difficulties is clear.

Transferring the Power of Choice to the Kids

Remember: **"That's one"** means that you are serious, minus lectures. It also puts the ball in the child or teen's court—minus arguing, threatening, sarcasm, or bribing. Putting the 3's chart in a visible spot seems like a very little thing. But it is often the little things that make a big difference. Sometimes older kids prefer that their charts not be in plain view when friends appear.

That's OK. The charts can be in a drawer and handy for checking as needed.

The Art of Consciously Disengaging From Difficulties

Using counting clues is an easy way to step away from the fray. **"That's one"** gets you on a reasonable road instead of one laden with justifiable but ineffective and intense emotion. There is a big difference between **"That's it. I've had it with your nonsense. I'm not paying any attention to you until you change your attitude"** and **"That's one. Nicer tone of voice please."**

The Parenting Path: Stay in Your Lane

Parenting paths are always bumpy, as there are no clear road maps to lead the way. Figuring out how to get past, over, and through these obstacles is essential. To do that, be sure to stick to the system steps.

COUNTING CLUES FOR
THE AGES 3 AND UNDER SET

*This wonderful group can respond very well to counting
clues even if they can't identify a one, a two, or a three.*

Adult response to a little one's choice to get to the sad 3 can
be: **"That's 3. Time-out"** or **"That's 3. Take space."** (Chapter 5)
This is an immediate response to a child's deciding to get the 3
and is meant to get the child's attention while at the same time
removing attention by the adult. A time-out is not only a take-a-
break, take-space for the child, but also for the adult.

There are a variety of ways to do an effective time-out. Details,
Cooperation Counts style, are described in Chapter 5.

Some little ones by age three are old enough to have an actual
3's chart along with the time-out or take-space strategies. It is

perfectly fine to have an immediate time-out at the count of three—along with a 3 on their chart, followed by a work-off at a later date. This will be a parental decision.

It is not advised to give counting clues to a child who is in "over-the-top" mode.

For all ages, let's remember that a time-out is just a time-out. Done properly, it is simply a take-space opportunity, not a be-all end-all resolution to a problem. It is not even meant to teach a "lesson." A time-out is really just meant to be a quick take-a-break time for everyone.

COUNTING CLUES FOR THE AGES 3–15 CROWD

Basically, the Cooperation Counts system revolves around the fact that if kids decide to get 3's, those 3's then belong to the adults and must be worked off. *A WORK-OFF WILL NOT BE A CHORE*. It is more like losing time from an event the child is eager to attend, or even losing the whole event. Adults are advised to be empathetic when implementing a work-off. The kids have the job of deciding to get the 3's or not. The adults have the sad job of getting them worked off (Chapter 2). When the consequence is completed, it is done. No lectures. Everyone moves on. Discussion might happen at a later time, but not in the heat of the moment.

All kids decide to get 3's and 3's are sad for the kids, even *very* sad, but there will be no permanent damage. Counting clues for the older set can be given in the form of "**First reminder, second reminder, that's 3,**" but I have found that the vocabulary used doesn't make much of a difference, although it is best to be consistent in your choice of phrases.

When NOT to Give Counting Clues or Work-Offs

It is not advised to give counting clues when a child is frightened or is in the middle of a tantrum, or to assign work-offs at bedtime. It is also best to do a work-off when you are not angry. The system's effectiveness resides in the beauty of waiting until everyone is calm. Sometimes ordinary conversation and checking in about an issue is enough to do the trick. If not, time warnings and counting clues can be considered.

SUMMARY

By using the Cooperation Counts tools, adults are out of the power struggles of "You will." "I won't! You can't make me!" We cannot *make* kids do something they don't *want* to do. We can, however, give them time warnings and counting clues so that the kids can decide what to do. Lecturing and yelling accomplish very little except perhaps to blow off some adult steam. Replacing frustration with time warnings and counting clues makes much more sense. Preserving dignity as well as much needed energy is a good thing.

As it turns out, those little numbers have big value for everyone!

CHAPTER 2
BASIC STEPS: WORK-OFFS OF 3'S

The Script: When something fun or important comes along, say, **"Let's check your chart. I see no 3's to work off. You're free and clear. Wonderful!"** or **"I see a 3. Hitting your brother on Tuesday. The work-off is......."** When the work-off is done, it is done. Move on!

Any 3's the kids decide to get belong to the adults and will need to be worked off. The kids' job is to decide to get the 3's or not. The adults' (sad) job is to get those 3's worked off. This is done by giving information that is read from the problem line on the chart and describing the work-off. Under most circumstances, kids do not decide or even participate in any discussion about what the work-off will be. Parents often wonder if Dad, for example, did the counting when his child chose to get a 3, does Dad need to be the one to do the work-off ? No. Any adult can get the work-off done.

WHAT IS A WORK-OFF?

A Work-Off is a Consequence, NOT a Punishment

A consequence needs to have two components:

1) The event or item chosen by the parent for the work-off must be very important to the child.

2) The event or item will—or will not—happen, no matter what the child says or does. He has control over the decision to get to the 3 in the first place, but does not have control over what the work-off is or when it will happen.

Getting the Kids' Attention

The point of a work-off is to get the kids' attention- that 3's are sad for them.

Fact

As of this writing, I know of no one who has ever expired from missing out on something special.

A Work-Off is NOT A CHORE!

Cleaning up a room, pulling weeds, doing something nice for a parent, neighbor, or even a sibling is **NOT** a work-off. Even doing a whole morning or night routine perfectly, when those scenes have previously been in the anything-but-perfect category, are not work-offs, because kids might or might not decide to do them, leading to a possible power struggle. In addition, these tasks are not usually important enough to most kids or teens. It is vital to get the kids' recognition that 3's mean trouble for them. Doing chores and helping out could (and most likely should) be stars (Chapter 3). A star is a star; a work-off is a work-off. It is crucial not to confuse the two. This distinction needs to be carefully observed.

No Work-Offs at Bedtime

It is not recommended to do a work-off at bedtime as that is a time to wind down, not to rev up.

How to Do an Effective Work-Off; Easy Script, Simple Steps.

"Let's Check Your Chart":

This is a very important phrase. For example, Bill is invited by Elizabeth to come over for pizza. If the answer could be yes and you agree, the next step would be to say in a matter-of-fact way,

"Let's check your chart."

Scene #1: **"I see no 3's to work off!" "Terrific! Hop into the car!"**

Scene #2: **"Oh no. I See a 3"** (or two or three 3's). Use a sad, empathetic, matter-of-fact tone of voice.

Avoid "You" have a 3. Stick with "**I** see a 3." This dodges any chance of being accusatory.

Read off the problem. This is important and is where lectures and lessons disappear, but the information about the poor choice is given. **"Teeth not brushed on Tuesday night."** Say nothing else. Think for a few seconds and then say something like: **"Oh, dear. No teeth brushing. Let's see.....the work-off is........waiting for fifteen minutes before going to Elizabeth's for pizza, *and the time starts when you are all settled down.*"**

Cheering for the Kids!

Cheer Bill on! Since this work-off is a consequence, not a punishment, parents are on the kids' side. They *want* the work-off to be done and over with! **"Great! It looks like the time can start now!"**

If there is Trouble, the Time Needs to Start Over Again

If Bill is complaining, say *calmly,* **"The time starts when you're settled down."** Translation: No fresh talk, rudeness, complaining, etc.

Watch for a quiet moment and say in an upbeat sort of way, **"Oh good! The time can start now."**

It is fine for Bill to do something else to pass the time. He is just doing a work-off of 3's by waiting to see Elizabeth and delaying the yummy pizza. After all, *he* had *decided* not to brush his teeth, but there will be no lectures.

If there is trouble, your response is only (sadly) **"Oh no, the time needs to start again."** Say nothing more at this time.

Keep to the Important "I" Messages

Avoid "You can't...." Say only: **"I see two 3's. No shower on Monday and rudeness on Wednesday. Hhhhhmmmmmm. The work-off is waiting for fifteen minutes to go to Elizabeth's house"**.

As the work-off of the fifteen minutes of waiting to go to Elizabeth's house continues, adults are encouraged do some more "cheering on": **"Only six more minutes to go." "Only two more minutes to go. Get your coat ready." "One more**

55

minute." "Done!" Great!" High five!

Visibility is Good; Arguing is Not

Write on the work-off line on the 3's chart (Chapter 1), "Waited 15 minutes to go to Elizabeth's house." A work-off is a work-off, not a debate about whether or not it was completed.

Date	Problem	Work-Off
5/18	3: Teeth not brushed	Waited 15 min. to see Elizabeth

Ending the Work-off: Time to Move On "Great! Good-bye 3! Hello Elizabeth!"

> *Getting the kids' attention is critical. Working off 3's and earning stars are two ways to do that and, I might add, allows for being respectful to the kids while doing so.*

More About Trouble

This could come in the form of a child of any age being rude, yelling, or making trouble during the work-off.

Say only, **"Oh no. The time needs to start again!"** and start it. No discussion. Let me repeat that: *No discussion!*

When the work-off is done, this is the time for jubilation, not lectures about the virtues of teeth brushing or anything else, for that matter. Focus on returning to the fun of normal life.

Using the clues in this way gives the power of choice to the kids about deciding whether or not to cooperate. The spotlight is no longer on the adults. Accepting consequences for their choices is completely with the kids.

About Empathy, Sympathy, Sadness, and Giving Information

Remember: Work-offs are done empathically, sympathetically, even sadly, in an informational tone of voice and using very few words. If the system steps are followed, there is no room for revenge or threats of any kind—empty or otherwise.

No Lectures Please!

Say in the direction of the 3 on the chart: **"Good-bye 3,"** or **"Done,"** or **"Phew!"** Write in the consequence on the work-off line. That's it!

The consequence has been accomplished without bribes, threats, criticism, or lectures. Forget phrases like "Now are you going to brush your teeth when you are asked?" "Was it worth it?" Erase them from your vocabulary PERMANENTLY! They accomplish nothing other than harm.

No Sea of 3's Please

A work-off can be worth one or more 3's. That is left to the discretion of the adults. It is not helpful for kids to see multiple 3's on the chart that have not yet been worked off. This can produce needless frustration, anxiety, and even "giving up." This is not the intent of the program. Work-offs do not need to coincide with the importance of the reason for which the child chose to get the 3; thus, both "no lollipop" and "no movie" fit the criteria of a work-off.

Examples of Work-offs

A ride: I often ask the kids, "Do you have your driver's license yet?" This makes it clear. If a child needs or wants to get somewhere, a car and a legal driver are required to get them there. So, not taking them or delaying taking them to a desired place can be a work-off. Then it's done. Drive on!

Computers need keyboards. Keyboards can disappear—but be sure to relocate it when the child is somewhere else. The keyboard could be temporarily placed in the trunk of a car or in a neighbor's house, as it needs to be made completely unavailable. When the work-off is done, it is done. The keyboard is returned and information is written on the work-off line. "No computer for two hours." It is done. Surf on!

Video games systems need controllers. These controllers can disappear. Actually, a work-off can be no screens at all. Upon completion of the work-off, it is done. Play on!

School dances need adults to make sure whoever is there is "legal." Arriving twenty minutes late is sad but when the work-off of a 3 (or several 3's) is done, it is done. Dance, dance, dance!

Concert tickets are expensive and often hard to come by. Part of the fun is going with the gang. Arriving in one's parents' car thirty minutes late is embarrassing and sad but not fatal. When a work-off is done, it is done. Hurry on in!

Hamburgers: A cashier at a fast-foods place will not serve a hamburger to a child without parental permission. If Cooperation Counts parents fear that starvation might set in, a less-desired but perfectly acceptable sandwich from home could be offered to replace the forbidden (for today) hamburger. If this nice gesture is rejected, empathy can certainly be shared—sincere empathy, of course, about the no-hamburger-today work-off. If a tantrum is the response to a work-off, that does not change the sad loss of the scrumptious hamburger. Sandwiches are nice!

A work-off can be as small as a **doughnut**, as long as it is important and will absolutely not get anywhere near the child's mouth. A work-off will happen no matter what. Adult giving-in is not an option. A work-off is a work-off. When it is done, it is. Good-bye, 3!

A dinner and a sleep-over invitation could turn into just the dinner part. Bon appetit!

Cell phones and minutes for the older crowd are usually in the category of "really important," but cell phones have been known to disappear. It doesn't take a rocket scientist to figure out that a cell phone that is unavailable is most definitely a work-off possibility—without threats or bribes, of course. It is just a work-off of a 3 (or 3's). There are no lectures, criticism or adult raised voices. There could be sympathetic voices, but that's it. Then, when the work-off is done, it is over. Keep on talking!

Heading for the Stars

Be sure to watch for star behavior for the child of any age who is doing well under difficult circumstances, or even for the work-off child who settles down quickly.

The Art of Waiting

To implement a work-off, give the information by reading off the problem area on the 3's chart. **"I see two 3's. Rude to Dad on Tuesday and wouldn't come in from outside on Wednesday. The work-off is... waiting for 10 minutes to go to the park (mall, etc), and the time starts when you are settled down."**

Mom is encouraged to head into "cheerleader" mode: **"Yes! The time starts now!"** For example, if her son starts calling Mom "mean," Mom's response should be *only*, **"Oh no. The time needs to start again."** She can, once again, cheer him on. After all, she is on his side—getting the work-off of those two 3's done and over with. When the ten minutes is over, write it on the chart and two 3's are worked off. Head for the park!

> *3's are definitely not in the fun category when it is work-off time, but the good news is that when they are worked-off, the 3's are gone. Adults: be aware of traps such as "I don't care" or "It doesn't make any difference to me." If there is any response from you at all (and that is questionable) it could be the age-old safe phrase such as **"Thank you for letting me know."** Period!*

An effective work-off involves *no* power struggles. Grabbing anything from a child is definitely out. Lollipops in hand or mouth, keyboards being used at the moment, and so on can be work-offs, but just not at that moment.

Avoiding Marshmallow Mode or Captain of the Ship Tones When It Is Work-Off Time; Always Follow Through

Implementing a work-off is where many parents have a tough time because follow-through often means a sad, mad, or even furious child—at least temporarily. The key word to keep in mind is "temporarily."

Please be aware of your tone of voice when reading a work-off. Too soft or too commanding tones will not do.

A sharing information tone is just right.

Most adults do not like to see their children in this non-cheerful mood, but even more usual is the worry that if the kids are upset with the adults, this somehow gets translated into fears such as: "Maybe my kids won't love me."

Often adults will worry, "Am I being too strict, the way my own parents were with me?" Using Cooperation Counts tools allows for the all-important follow-through when the kids' choice is not to cooperate with a request or rule. In truth, kids and teens have been given time warnings, a round of counting clues, and then perhaps even another round—plenty of time to decide whether or not they are going to cooperate.

Stay on Track

This is where adults often lose their grip and give in. This spells trouble. The kids might even try to put the "bad-guy hat" on the adults, but this will not work if the steps of the program are followed.

So, check the chart, be brave, get the work-off done and over with, and a whole lot is accomplished. Check the chart even if there are no 3's that need to be worked off. **"I don't see any 3's. You are 3-free!"**

Do Not Preview the Work-off

It is usually advised that the specifics of a work-off not be discussed prior to the time of the consequence. This is done for many reasons including that it is not usually much fun for anyone to hear whining and complaining for long periods of time. For example, if a work-off were to be discussed a week in advance, this might lead to having to listen to multiple reasons about why "It isn't fair," "You're mean," etc. The etceteras can get annoying and loud. This is not healthy for anyone.

Special Circumstances

Under some circumstances, kids can know what a work-off might be. For example, **"The work-off of each 3 will be losing one more day of the cell phone."** This is not said in a threatening or angry tone. It is just information.

Start Them Out Easy: Work-offs are Meant to Get the Kids' Attention

The severity or length of time of a work-off is not the focus. The importance is that the work-off has been done at all. While a work-off can be anywhere from waiting a few minutes to losing the whole event, losing the entire event should be considered only after it is clear that the kids are continuing to decide not to cooperate over a period of time.

Self-Reflective Adults

Even if there are multiple times when kids decide not to co-operate by one or by two, it is important to consider reasons why this might be happening. You can look at your own tone of voice and expectations, the time of day of requests, whether or not the kids are tired or hungry. Has it been a hard day fraught with frustrations? Have there been important disappointments?

Ask yourself: Is this a time to offer comfort instead of making a request?

A Word about Robots

Parenting is not about expecting the kids to swing into robot mode "Because I said so." This simply will not work for anyone, anytime.

Discipline Done Respectfully

Giving the kids chances for their choices (time warnings, counting clues) is a respectful way to let the kids know when the adults are serious. Work-offs provide consistent follow-through, the operant word being *CONSISTENT*.

Leaving the Troubles Behind

Using the system provides the wonderful component of moving on, leaving the troubles behind. Stars (Chapter 3) provide the opportunity for praising wonderful choices. Healthy adult/child relationships need a balance of discipline and praise with follow-through in both areas. Using the Cooperation Counts steps accomplishes all of that.

If there is any discussion at all about the original issue leading to the choice of getting the 3, it should be at another time when everyone is calm. **"Remember the night you didn't want to sit at the table for dinner?"** If your child is willing to discuss it, that's fine but the 3 has been worked off. It is done. End of story.

The Mystery of the Missing 3's Charts

Sometimes it happens that 3's charts go missing, or may even be discovered in crumpled or torn condition in illegal places. No problem. If this situation occurs, the adults will try hard to remember which 3's had been worked off and which 3's had not. Unfortunately, all of the 3's that had already been worked off may not be able to be recalled exactly, and any 3's on the new chart would, very sadly of course, need to be worked off.

About Adult Dignity

By using these simple tools, adult dignity remains in place—a difficult task made simple.

Rearranging the Power

We are now giving the power to the kids—the power they've had all along—to make their own choices. Giving time warnings and counting clues is how the rearrangement of power happens. The children learn that a poor choice leads to a consequence. Some children decide to accumulate a large number of 3's consistently over time. This is important information for parents who are looking for thoughtful ways to identify and address areas of difficulty.

The Goal is Not Zero 3's

The focus is on the children's choices. They do not need to get 3's if they don't want to; however, the goal is *not* zero 3's, as all children will decide to get them at various times.

3's Always Mean There Will Be Work-Offs

The goal is to help kids make thoughtful choices by thinking first, acting later, managing impulsiveness, deciding for themselves what to do, and accepting the consequences (both positive and negative) of their behaviors, without a single adult lecture. Each child will decide whether or not to get 3's. It's just that simple.

When you use these parental strategies, you avoid a state of exhaustion while taking a huge load off your shoulders. The outcome of the request to cooperate or not is now **up to the child.** This leads to fewer power struggles, which leaves room for added parenting interventions that can offer chances to have even better outcomes in the parent-child interactions of daily life. You can now work less and relax more.

Dreams Can Come True

Emotional relaxation is often only a dream when facing multiple daily dilemmas in the parenting department. Now we have a chance to make those dreams come true!

When NOT to Give Counting Clues or Work-Offs

It is not advised to give counting clues when a child is frightened or is in the middle of a tantrum, or to assign work-offs at bedtime. It is also best to do a work-off when the adult is not angry. The system's effectiveness resides in the beauty of waiting until everyone is calm. Sometimes ordinary conversation and checking in about an issue is enough to do the trick. If not, time warnings and counting clues can be considered.

A NO-COUNTING CLUES OPTION: WHERE'S TIM?

As previously addressed, conversation is always an option. We are not looking for robot mode, with kids being expected to hop to it "because I said so."

The family rule was simple. Come home after school by 3:00 and check-in with Mom or Dad. There had been no trouble until one Wednesday afternoon. Three o'clock came. No Tim. Time marched on. Still no Tim. There was no answer on his cell phone. Both parents rapidly went from calm to panicked. By 3:15, Mom and Dad were in touch with each other. Mom hopped into her car while simultaneously calling Tim's friends and found that he was not with any of them. By 3:45, Mom and Dad were loudly disagreeing with each other. Dad's take was, "He's probably just fine." Mom's take was to be furious at Dad for even entertaining such a notion. At 3:50, in walked Tim.

"What happened? Where were you?" was the obvious question to Tim. Dad's tone was fairly casual. Mom's was not.

"I was hanging up posters at school with my science teacher," said the calm and surprised-looking Tim.

In our family therapy session, this scene was addressed from a variety of viewpoints. Mom thought Tim should get an automatic 3, since this was a violation of their long-standing rule, which was in place for safety. Dad thought it was "just a guy thing. He's fine, so let's not worry about it for now." This is a prime scene specifically made for marital discord.

Everyone ultimately agreed that since there had been no *pattern* of disappearing after the 3:00 check-in rule, a conversation was in order. "I knew where I was" got Mom *and* Dad's blood pressure up a bit, but when encouraged to consider the big picture as well as the little picture, they decided it made more sense to go the conversation route first. Tim did not get an automatic 3—this time. He agreed that just because *he* knew where he was did not mean that his frantic parents did.

They all made a clear family rule: If a plan changes, discuss it right away.

Problem-solving can always be considered as a reasonable first choice, but a *pattern* of not showing up on time is different. This is when having a clear plan in place—like using time warnings, counting clues, work-off's and stars—can be a lifesaver. Otherwise, enjoy using creativity for the just-right position of the special science posters!

69

SUMMARY

Any 3's the kids decide to get are noted in the box on the 3's chart and dated. The problem is stated on one line; the work-off is stated on the next line, upon its completion.

When it is time for a work-off, say **"Let's check your chart."** Read off the problem and then say, **"The work-off is......"** Refrain from using the phrase "You can't......"

When the 3's are worked off, move on. Enjoy the kids and head for the stars! Even when you are serious, it may sometimes be preferable to first address the matter via a conversation. If not, time warnings, counting clues, and work-offs are always an option.

CHAPTER 3

BASIC STEPS: STARS

What is a Star?

A star is praise made visible. Noticing an effort to change behaviors that had previously been anything but positive is essential.

> *There are whole websites devoted to the theme, "Catch them doing something right." Praise from parents is as important as the discipline. Praising is fun. Don't be shy!*

How to Get a Star

Stars are given by the adults who notice kids' efforts to make positive choices. Stars are not just for the younger set. Stars are very valuable for the older set as well. Ten stars equal something nice. The something nice is not a trip to Disney World, but there are lots of nice things that could be agreed upon by everyone. If there is a reward system already in place, it can stay, be replaced with a Cooperation Counts chart or with one that is offered as an "original" by a family member of any age.

Stars Stay; They Don't Go Away

Even if disaster strikes immediately after earning a star, the star stays.

Stars do not work-off 3's. Stars are stars, 3's are 3's.

Let's say that Lance has decided to turn off the TV by one or by two—or even with no counting clues at all. This is a great chance for the adults to notice his valiant effort. **"Lance, thanks so much for turning off the TV. I know that wasn't easy for you. Wonderful! It's time for a star! Congratulations!"**

Circle the star and date it. Write on the line next to the star, "Turned off the TV."

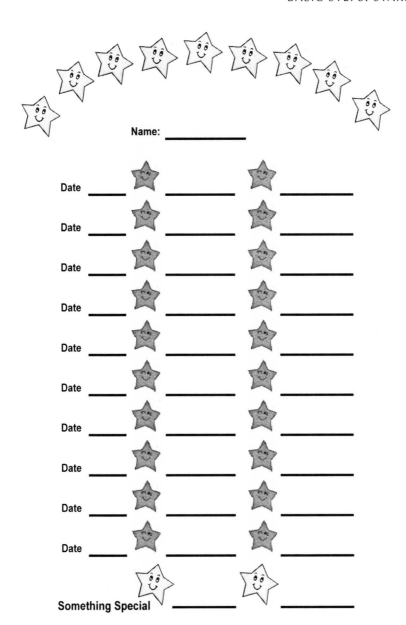

Name: _____

Date _____

Date _____

Date _____

Date _____

Date _____

Date _____

Date _____

Date _____

Date _____

Date _____

Something Special _____

Keep an Eye Out for Opportunities to Give Stars

A game has begun. Give information first. **"We don't know who will win or lose, but I'm watching for star behavior either way."** Then, if a child usually cries when he doesn't win, watch for an opportunity to give a star when he is able to 'keep it together' or even if his choice is to voluntarily take space especially when he is upset.

Stars can be given for each event, or adults can watch for a pattern of positive behaviors and effort

If work-offs are done well, this could equal a star. We want to compliment the wonderful world of self-control and positive choices. This is one way to do it.

If a child decides to cooperate by one or by two or even without counting clues, this could lead to a star.

Notice if there are no 3's for a period of time. Star!

Be creative. Here is where adults can encourage family and personal values, effort, anger management, courage, and difficult but appropriate choices.

Noticing star behaviors and choices is vitally important. Notice the positives as a parental priority. There is no limit to the number of stars that can be earned in any time period.

Ten Stars Equals Something Nice

The child can make a suggestion, but the adults need to OK it. Some kids will be sure of their goal but by star #8 or #9 or even by star #10 they may decide on something different. No problem. Kids do not have a say about a work-off. But they definitely can suggest their Gold Star Treat and the adults will let them know if they agree. Write the treat on the chart after it has happened.

Setting Up a Special Wall of Stars

Along with using the star charts, how about making some additional stars, filling in the date along with the good deed, and hanging them up! This wall of stars can mirror the stars on the chart, but even if a very young child doesn't yet have a star chart, visible, showy (even sparkly) stars can draw attention to good choices.

Possible treats—Let the Kids get Creative

- An outing
- Money
- A doughnut
- Special time with an adult, sibling, or friend,.
- Choosing and eating a dessert—for breakfast
- Deciding the menu for dinner
- Inviting a friend to visit

- Cell phone minutes
- A sleep-over
- "Taking" the family bowling
- Picking out a movie for a family night
- A toy, jelly beans, or ice cream
- A trip to the mall (dollar amount stated)

Begging for Stars

Once kids discover the value of stars, they often beg for them. This is a typical response and can be handled in clear, respectful, encouraging ways. They may ask, "Is this a star?" If it is, say yes and get it on the chart. If not, share encouragement. **"You're doing great! I'm watching for when you get ready on time in the morning, and I'll be sure to let you know when it is star time."**

Manipulation?

"My child is just manipulating me by asking if she can unload the dishwasher when she has always avoided that job like the plague!" So be it. I encourage you to thank her, and let her know you will be looking forward to peeking into an empty dishwasher. Please remember to compliment her on a job well done and what a help she was.

What Do Stars Have to Do With Impulsivity?

Surprisingly, stars can have a lot to do with impulsivity. Let's say that a child or teen escalates from OK to furious in the blink of an eye. In daily life, this is seen in various ways, which can include kicking, biting, verbally fighting, punching, throwing things, screaming, or scratching. Everyone around the suddenly violent child of any age is at a loss as to what to do.

Of course, any violent act is an automatic 3, belongs to the adults, and will need to be worked off at an appropriate time (Chapter 2). Let's keep in mind that giving counting clues to a child involved in a tantrum is completely ineffective, but safety for everyone is a must. This includes for the impulsively violent one as well as everyone around him. Violence as a way of handling intense emotion is "against the law" everywhere. Period.

Cooperation Counts parents are quickly trained, however, to notice the positives. Go for it! Use the power of those stars to notice when a child of any age might have escalated—and didn't—even by accident. **"Wow! I just saw that when the dog knocked over your special lego structure, you didn't hurt anyone. You screamed at the top of your lungs BUT YOU DIDN'T HURT ANYONE. Way to go! That's a wonderful star. Actually, that is definitely a double star choice. Do you want me to help with the lego damage?"**

Even if there is an escalation that follows, the stars stay. They were earned and are included with the other stars. This one might read "self-control when the legos fell."

This sort of "watching for the stars" is critical and can even help to focus on the goal of helping kids and adults manage their own anger. Insisting on noticing the positives is one way to accomplish this complex goal.

Focusing on Trouble Spots; Noticing Turn-Arounds via the Stars (Pouncing on the Positives)

If failing to get dressed promptly, get hair brushed, arguing with adults/siblings, forgetting things in school, making everybody late in the morning, homework hassles, or bedtime blues have been particularly bothersome scenes, when the scene is turned around, head for the stars!

MORNING MADNESS:PART II
STAR STYLE

Let's say that Molly, Ken, and Sandy all decided to get into the car on time. Let's say that time warnings along with counting clues were given and the kids decided to cooperate by one, by two, or even before. They are golden! They could each be given a star. In the line to the right of the star will be written **"In the car on time for school."** Ten stars equals something nice. Way to go, Molly, Ken, and Sandy!

Dad now cheers for the kids. He is not rendered helpless if Sandy (or anyone) decides not to cooperate, but party mode prevails if the morning exit goes smoothly. The big picture involves thousands of times of leaving the house on time for work and for school. Let's see what the kids decide—minus adult lectures.

When adults are less stressed, that helps everything.

Using the Star Chart as a Confidence Builder

"Lets take a look at your star chart" is a wonderful way to heap on praise that is a big part of encouraging kids to want to try to do their best and is a quick and an easy way to highlight having overcome a particular challenge. Here are some samples:

"Made Edna smile when she was sick."
"Fed the dog."
"Got dressed quickly."
"Put groceries away without being asked."
"Got into the car to go to school on time."
"Shared the last candy bar with Ben."
"Didn't fight with Zack all day."
"Stayed in bed all night."
"Helped with the laundry."
"Did homework without being reminded."
"Came in on time."
"Had nice manners at dinner."
"Left the park without a fuss."
"Didn't use rude talk when mad."
"Stayed in bed for three nights in a row."

"Read books for a long time."
"Stayed at the lunch table for the whole time."
"No 3's all day."

The star chart becomes very powerful when parents add some interpretation: **"That was very brave of you to try a new food."**

The star chart is definitely a confidence booster—for the adults as well as for the kids: **"He did it!" "I did it!"**

> *Watching for stars is a wonderful way to encourage busy parents to put conscious effort into "noticing the nice." Positive messages can be given just by reading the star chart.*

Turn Them Into Movie Stars

In the spirit of 'catch them doing something right,' how about using a camcorder or even a camera or cell phone to record positive moments? Keep a device handy and when your child is helping out, cleaning up, smiling at a brother or sister, these are the moments we want to capture. A movie night featuring Judy and Joe making good choices could be a big hit!

SUMMARY
Setting Everyone Up for Success:
A Win/Win Situation

Watching for star behaviors is fun and, as it turns out, is highly recommended. The star charts may be for the kids and teens, but the power of using stars as part of the Cooperation Counts program comes from the adults' willingness to notice kids' positive behaviors. Please give stars often. At first, to encourage kids and teens to do their best, stars may be given very frequently, but it is also acceptable to notice *patterns* of cooperation which then lead to the stars. When parents are watching for positive choices, it also helps to set themselves up for more successful relationships with each other as well as with the kids. This is clearly a win/win situation.

THOSE LITTLE STARS CAN BE EXTREMELY POWERFUL!

CHAPTER 4
TIDBITS

STICKY SCHOOL CONNECTIONS

Mom and Dad picked up Kyle from preschool, where they made the sad discovery that he had decided to leave the playground without permission. This is a Cooperation Counts family, and so they asked the teacher for a sticky. On it, they wrote a big 3 and under it wrote "Left the playground at school." They stuck it onto the dashboard of the car and picked up their other two kids. On the way home, they stopped at a store.

The stop at this particular store was no accident. It was a well known fact that the best donuts in the world were located there, and the kids knew it. The parents had looked meaningfully at each other when the school 3 sticky was being written. They had nodded silently to each other.

Dad parked the car. Mom asked who would like to come in with her and while in the store, get connected with the delightful donuts. All three kids were ecstatic! Mom said simply, **"Great. Abby and Nate, we know you have no 3's to work off. Wonderful! Oh, Kyle, I see the school 3."** She peered carefully at the sticky dangling from the dashboard and read it aloud. **"Oh dear. Leaving the school playground without permission. Phooey! The work-off is missing going into the store. That means no donut. Oh no!"** Please note: Mom did not say "You can't have a donut because you didn't follow the playground rules." That's because she didn't want the spotlight to be on her, which most likely would have made her the bad-guy. She was just sadly letting him know what the work-off of leaving-the-school-playground 3 would be. There were no lectures or trying to teach any lessons, which would likely have fallen on uninterested ears. Mom and the two kids went into the store.

Kyle started to wail—REALLY LOUDLY. Dad waited and when he could get a word in between the REALLY, REALLY LOUD WAILING, he shared how sad this was not being able to have the delectable donut, and thank goodness that the school 3 would be all worked-off and done with. Mom and the kids came back into the car, wiping off crumbs as they got into their seats. Kyle wailed louder! Mom and Dad reminded the other kids that they were watching for star behaviors, which would be based on paying absolutely no attention to the screaming Kyle.

The good news is that Kyle lived through this ordeal. The sticky was actually torn up and thrown away. It was done. And there is more good news. The next day, when Kyle was picked up from school, his parents were given the good news that he'd had a great day, even on the playground. You know where they were delighted to head before going home—and they all joyously ate donuts. Rather than lecturing Kyle, they partied instead.

CINDY AND THE SPEECH THERAPIST

Cindy needed to see a speech and language therapist and her parents had found a wonderful one. The problem was that Cindy was not interested, even though her parents and teachers definitely were. Testing clearly identified deficits that could easily be addressed by a speech specialist. Everything was in place except for the fact that Cindy refused to participate. Multiple strategies were tried, but there was no change. Although the therapist made the sessions lively and interesting, still no go. The parents were frustrated, the therapist was out of tricks, and Cindy continued to resist.

As these non-productive speech therapy sessions continued to be non-productive, it so happened that the Cooperation Counts program was introduced to Cindy and her family. Within a few days, Cindy had been well trained. She now had the power to decide to cooperate with her adults—or not. She loved the fact that she could decide. Her parents loved the fact that they didn't need to work so hard at trying to get Cindy to do what they asked. Whether she chose to cooperate or not, her parents remained consistent by sticking with the steps.

Thursday rolled around and once again it was time for another session.

Cindy's parents quickly explained the system to the speech therapist. Basically, she was told about time warnings, counting clues, 3's, work-offs, and stars. It was agreed that any 3's Cindy decided to get in her session would be transferred to her home chart and would need to be worked off, while star behaviors would also be noted.

This turned out to be a wonderful session since Cindy decided to cooperate with the therapist, who, as usual, had prepared a fun lesson. That was it. Subsequent sessions continued to be productive.

Getting Cindy's attention with the Cooperation Counts tools had clearly turned out to have multiple benefits for everyone.

THE WEDDING STORY

Sherry was nine and had a mind of her own. She was born that way and everyone knew it. She was the youngest of five; her four older brothers were now adults and leading success-ful lives. Then, along came Sherry. Mom and Dad had always thought of themselves as experienced, confident parents, but that was "before Sherry."

For years, Ms. Sherry ruled the roost. This was not a secret; it was the awful truth. She did fine in school, but the word "fine" did not apply at home, not even close.

Finally, Mom and Dad became Cooperation Counts parents—just in time, as it turned out. The system was put into place and wonder of wonders, Mom and Dad cooled down and continued to use the program on a daily basis. At first, it was clear: Sherry decided to get to 3 regularly. The system was followed carefully. Mom and Dad were cool as cucumbers. When it was time for something fun, "Let's Check Your Chart" was in place and work-offs were important, but once done, they were over and done with. Within a week, they began to notice something: The old pattern was being reversed. Sherry was deciding to cooperate by one or by two, she was deciding not to get very many 3's, and her star chart had lines and lines of stars. Any 3's she decided to get were worked-off with fewer high drama meltdowns.

Now, here is why, at the beginning of this true story, I used the words "just in time." Big brother Bud was going to get married. There was going to be a traditional ceremony and party, but sadly, they all agreed that Sherry could not be included. It was just too risky. She might do just about anything to ruin this important event. She had never blinked an eye about a display of emotions in public. Bud and the family just couldn't chance it, not at this most important of celebrations.

Then they noticed that Sherry was doing the big turn-around. She stayed in that mode for several weeks. It wasn't too late to order her special dress, and they still didn't have a replacement for the all-important jobs of flower girl and ring bearer. Sherry got the dress, got the two jobs, and decided to behave beautifully during the ceremony: When some of the flowers spilled, she just picked them up without a fuss. That was worth a lot of stars!

Time has passed. There is a plan in place when Sherry decides to cooperate, as well as when she doesn't. Her parents are back to enjoying parenting again. All is well in times of trouble as well as in times of peace.

TRASH NEWS
THE TALE OF THE TORN-UP 3'S CHART

Cooperation Counts parents often come up with ingenious ways to deal with difficulties. This, like all of the others in this book, is a true story.

Joe, age nine, was not happy about the Cooperation Counts system. He liked the way things used to be much better. His parents used to give in a lot. All Joe needed to do was to get loud, and that usually did it. Cooperation Counts changed all of that. Joe hated 3's! He hated work-offs! He didn't even care about stars. Let's face it. He hated the fact that it was up to him to decide to cooperate or not. He'd show his Mom and Dad a thing or two. So he tore up his 3's chart into a million pieces and threw it into the trash.

Later that afternoon, Joe's friend called to ask if he would like to join his family to play miniature golf. Indeed he did! His parents said that would be fine and then said the usual: **"Let's Check Your Chart."** No problem this time, thought Joe. The chart was all torn up, but to quote Joe at our session, "Mom put my friend's mom on hold while she pulled out the millions of pieces. What was she doing? She was wasting time by putting all of the little pieces of the stupid 3's chart together. It took forever! Finally, she told my friend's mom that we would need to call her back and she wasted more time with all those little pieces."

Finally, she got the chart together and said, **"I see a 3. Hitting your brother on Wednesday afternoon. The work-off is..... no miniature golf today."**

Joe was shocked. "Whatever happened to the waiting for five minutes to go golfing? THIS IS ABSOLUTELY NOT FAIR!"

His Mom said only, **"This is very sad. I hope there will be another chance for you to go with your friend. Hitting is an automatic 3 and it has happened several times recently."**

After Joe recovered from the shock and outrage of it all, this is what he finally came up with:

"I am the one who can decide about stuff. I'd love to hit my brother because he usually deserves it, but I'm not going to let my ding-dong brother get in the way of fun with my friends. I hope my friend will ask me to do something fun again. Actually, I think I'll call him up and ask him about that."

The work-off was done. End of the sad story. Beginning of a new chapter. The next day, Mom even helped Joe to get something special going with his friend. Happy ending!

MORE TRASH NEWS;
SETTING UP THE KIDS FOR SUCCESS

One smart Cooperation Counts family decided enough was enough with trouble about the trash can. Jared, age six, always seemed to be in (and on) the one in the kitchen—illegally, so they put their heads together and figured out what to do. They decided to put a great big red 3 on the top of the outlawed area. If Jared decided to go into (or on) it without permission, that was an automatic 3. If he remained cooperative about the no-getting-into-the-trash-can rule, stars came his way. That big red 3 turned out to be a big help!

"BUT NOBODY WILL LISTEN IF I DON'T YELL!"

Stephanie is the proud grandmother of three teen grandchildren. She is also raising them. In her family, yelling had been an accepted way of life for generations. When she first heard about the Cooperation Counts program, which included replacing yelling with time warnings and counting clues, she insisted that keeping the shouting to an absolute minimum was not for her. She was a yeller and she would always remain so. She was raised that way, and anyway, the kids would never listen to her if she didn't yell. She admitted that most of the time they didn't pay much attention to her anyway, but letting go of yelling was completely out of the question.

Stephanie never bought into using the full Cooperation Counts system, but something did click with the no-yelling part. She gave it a try and discovered that the kids paid more attention to her when she wasn't screaming at them. She practiced some more and decided that she did not need to be screeching. "Just because I've been screaming and yelling forever, doesn't mean that it's right. It doesn't mean I can't decide to make some changes, and I'm glad I did!" As an added benefit, someone else was happy about all of this—her doctor. As it turns out, Stephanie's blood pressure actually went down!

IN AND OUT

On Tuesday, Dad decided to take both daughters to the supermarket after school. Sandra, age six, had some significant developmental delays. Her nine-year-old sister Tabitha did not. Traditionally, store scenes were difficult with a capital "D," so they were avoided. The culprit was Sandra, but the combination of the two girls in a store together was not a pretty sight.

Cooperation Counts had been successfully put into place at home, but the dreaded store scenes had continued to be avoided in order to preserve Dad's sanity. The no-two-girls-in-the-store situation was, however, interfering with daily life. He finally decided to follow the program steps and adjusted his goal from "must get the milk" to thinking of the trip to the store as a "training mission" instead.

As advised, the rules were discussed with the girls, as preparation at each step—leaving the house, car behavior, before entering the store, in the store, etc. This was done in an informational way and using very few words.

At the store, they went in through the door, and literally back out again! Sandra had spotted the candy machines by the entrance and wanted some. She threw herself on the floor, and started screaming. Since giving time warnings and counting clues are "out" during a tantrum, Dad said only **"No screaming in the store, that's three. Time-out"** and they all left the store, Tabitha under her own steam along with loudly objecting Sandra. Dad propelled Sandra out and, of course, said nothing more to the screamer.

They went directly home, but with the screamer screaming loudly and the non-screamer being cheered on for her cooperation under such terrible circumstances. In fact, Tabitha earned a star for her excellent choices during the nasty scene.

Dad could have given Sandra a chance by announcing: **"That's 3, time-out" or even "That's 3, take space"** and proceeded outside for a chance to re-group. However, the ongoing non-pleasant store scenes had disrupted their daily lives so drastically and for so long that he was not in the mood to give much leverage, thus the departure.

At home, Sandra eventually settled down—with no attention having been paid to her during the loudness, of course. A 3 was entered, and under the "problem" line on her chart was written,

"Screaming in the store." The work-off line was left blank waiting for a consequence. There was no discussion at that time.

On Wednesday, Sandra was invited to play at a neighbor's house, the chart was checked, the 3 about screaming in the store was read aloud and the 3 was worked off by not playing with the (favorite, by the way) friend. Sandra was devastated—and so was Dad—but they tried to make the best of it by having a popsicle party. Yes, there was a sweet treat. No, there was not a special friend in sight.

On Thursday, Dad took both girls to the Garden Center. They were wonderful! Stars accumulated. Even if either of the girls had decided to act up, Dad was no longer rendered helpless. 3's would be charted, there would be a work-off that was important, and that would be that. The end.......no, actually the beginning of lots of outings together.

A STAR PARTY WITH TRIPLETS PLUS ONE

Mary is the divorced mother of four-year-old triplets and their almost six-year-old big brother. Mary was aware that for her large crew and circumstances there would be times when she would need to do some fancy adapting when it came to the Cooperation Counts methods. So she did. For example, try as she might, documenting 3's and stars accurately and promptly was often difficult. She had a cell phone, but no other technological device (Chapter 8). She did, however, keep a small notebook in her pocket and divided it into four sections—one for each child—to keep track of 3's, stars, and work-offs, which, under the often chaotic circumstances, was nothing short of amazing.

Mary found that it was not practical—or even safe—to follow the very short time-outs by removing the kids and her attention, so she just used the part about removing her own attention from them, quickly asking if they were all set. Work-offs were often group work-offs.

But then there were the all important stars. Here's what Miracle Mama cooked up.

Each night, she gathered the children, got out a special drink, gave everyone a fun cup and began the **Special Star Party**. This was a time for the children to be able to notice something nice that someone else had done for them during the day. The rules were that everyone would be very quiet, listen to the person with the compliment, and then everyone would "toast" the person who told the star story, as well as the person who had been the "star."

This became a nightly ritual and the kids began to look for things to compliment each other about at the party. Mary smiled from ear to ear as she enjoyed the stories. She also noticed that during the day, the kids were kinder towards one another, and she was always watching for ways to praise them.

At the Star Party, stories included such delightful contributions as:

"I hurt my finger and Mom was busy, so my brother told me he would wait with me until Mom could come." Then came the special toasts and the HOORAYs, as it would be flirting with danger to combine toasting and clapping!

"My sister put her arm around me when I was so sad." There were more toasts followed by enthusiastic HOORAYs.

Indeed, there are many ways to head for positive parenting. There are endless ways to create star opportunities, but one thing is for sure. Praising the kids is always fun, and good for everyone!

THE WRETCHED ROOM DISASTER

Abigail, age fourteen, was in her fourth foster home placement. Life had not treated her well in the past, and there had been multiple tragedies over the years. One issue had remained the same wherever she landed. Her room was always a mess. This was not the kind of mess with a small "m." This was a huge mess with a capital "M"! She prided herself on the fact that she had driven a number of people crazy with this issue. And so it was that the mess in her room grew into the intolerable category. She was happy enough with this placement, but she was not about to clean up her room under any circumstance.

Her foster family learned the Cooperation Counts methods and the system was put into place. A big event for Abigail was the annual bowling party, which was sponsored by the agency responsible for her. She wanted to go badly. Word had it that a boy who had been placed with a family across the state and whom she had met at last year's party was going to be there. The bowling party was more than an hour's drive away. She really wanted to go. Could it be that she wanted to see the favored far-away friend? Her foster Mom was eager to go to the bowling party, too, as she was going to spend time with other foster families, and she was really looking forward to that.

But there was the matter of that very messy room.

Abigail was given three days to clean it up. The room check was going to be at 2:00 on the day of the bowling party. Departure time was set for 2:15. Abigail did not have a driver's license. She wanted to get to the party. Her foster Mom wanted to take her. Abigail could not get to the party without her.

Abigail knew that her foster mom meant business. There were no threats, nagging, bribes, or lectures. There was hardly any discussion at all. Abigail decided she didn't want to chance not being able to go to the bowling party. She decided to clean up her room, but she waited until the last possible moment. Her foster Mom said nothing, except to give her a time warning of fifteen minutes. On the stroke of 2:00 the inspection was done.

It was a miracle! The room was completely cleaned up. Abigail had decided to do it. Everyone high-fived and off they went to the party. If the outcome of the room condition had been different, there would have been (sadly, of course) no bowling party, and Abigail knew it. She would have been working off a 3 instead of rolling the bowling ball with her friends and being able to gaze at the cute boy. The choice was given to Abigail, and it turns out that Abigail made a wonderful choice. Fun was had by all.

Note that the thread running through all of these stories is the consistency shown by every adult using the system. Cooperation Counts reigns!

CHAPTER 5

BASIC STEPS: TANTRUM AND TIME-OUT TIPS FOR THE YOUNGER SET

For Ages Two to Five

Parents often wonder how young is too young to begin "I mean business" mode. I believe that many children, often by the age of eighteen months or so, can get the message when their adults are serious.

Tantrum Tips

Think of a tantrum as being like a real fire. To make a fire bigger, just add fuel.

I believe that the fuel for a tantrum is attention. The solution? Remove the attention. **Don't look, don't talk, and don't touch.**

If the tantrum continues, you can check in with the child by saying (brightly), **"Are you all set?"** and then add, **"Are you all set for no hitting?"** (or identifying what the original problem was). I do not believe that a child needs to be completely settled down in order to be all set. A little nod, crying instead of screaming can all be signs of settling. If the child is not all set, go back to don't look, don't talk, don't touch and say the phrase, **"I see you're not all set"**, leave the room and frequently check in using only those specific phrases.

You may want to do something to help settle the scene, but there is really nothing that you can do effectively when your child is having a tantrum. Fueling the "fire" with attention usually just makes the "flames" bigger, so waiting until the upset child is done (at least done enough) and checking in with just one phrase, **"I see you're not all set to...."** turns out to be the biggest help after all.

If any child or adult is really upset, it does not help to offer advice such as, "Calm down" "It's not all that bad," "You'll get over it," "You're too loud." It just plain doesn't work. Waiting for the storm to pass is what makes sense and respects the fact that when emotions are over the top, they are simply....over the top. Tantrums can be loud for varying periods of time—from a few moments on up. But giving counting clues when a child is in the throes of a tantrum is not advised.

The Power of Popcorn and other Attention Getters!

Children decide to be all set under some interesting circumstances which might include smelling freshly made popcorn, hearing through the closed door that the family is getting ready to begin a movie, or that pizza has arrived. It's amazing but true. Being ready to end a tantrum can happen under VERY interesting circumstances.

Applause, Applause!

When a tantrum is over, we need to welcome back, enthusiastically, the no-longer-loud child. This may be a test for the non-relaxed adult who has just been in close proximity to the opposite of a peaceful interaction. Nevertheless, it is important to get a grip and do the welcoming. This can be done with a hug, a smile, high-five, thumbs up, wiping away tears, offering a snack. The focus is encouraged to be on the "all done" part of a tantrum. This is no time to try to teach a lesson and make sure it is learned. In fact, the opposite is true. A settled child has a better chance of staying settled when the adult is calm and ready to move on.

Tantrums in Public

Removing a child—quickly—is effective and often appreciated by those trying to make purchases, or eat a meal, while the removal also serves to get a child's attention.

In public, when a child is raging and the adult is not, there may be those in the "audience" who appear to be staring, looking critical or even downright horrified. However, there will also be those who show great respect for the non-reacting parent. This is, after all, quite a feat and will be admired by many onlookers, especially those who have had experience in this never-any-fun situation.

TIME-OUT TIPS

Getting the Kids' Attention

For this age group, simply removing adult attention can be very powerful.

Time-Out, Cooperation Counts Style: The Focus is on the 3

It is important to link the time-out with the 3, thus heading the spotlight away from the adult and avoiding the "punisher/bad guy" role.

I believe that a time-out is just a time-out. It is not a be-all, end-all. It is an immediate response to when a child decides to get to three. It is also a take-space, get settled down, take a breather time—for everyone. If a 3's chart is in place, keep in mind that a time-out does not work off a 3.

When to introduce work-off of 3's is a parental decision but can generally be put into place by the time a child is about four years old.

Location, Location

An effective time-out place needs to be where there is the least likelihood of power struggles and attention *from anyone*. A room with a door is ideal. Toys in the room is just fine.

The Time-Out Script:

"In two minutes, it will be time to put your bowl in the sink."

"In one minute, it will be time to put your bowl in the sink."

"Almost time…"

"Now it's time. Bowl in the sink, please." Use only a very few words and say *nothing* else. Wait for three seconds, then give counting clues (Chapter 1) in a calm, informational voice.

If the decision is to cooperate by one or by two, great!

If not, say after two only, **"No bowl in the sink. That's 3, time-out."**

If a time-out (with adult involvement) is any longer than about ten seconds, it could happen that the kids get into the space of "Hey, this is cool. I can keep my Mom holding the doorknob for a really long time." Preventing the adult from being held hostage is critical to the time-out process and, after all, holding the doorknob is also a form of attention.

Removing Adult Attention

I do not believe that an effective time-out means chasing a child anywhere. Removing attention means no talking to the timed-outer: NO talking, NO looking, and NO touching other than taking the loud one to the time-out place or holding her firmly—away from eye contact, of course.

When a Time-Out is Done: Clap, Cheer, Hug, High-Five

Disengage. Then re-engage. When a time-out is done, it is over. Good-bye to grudges. A pleasant **"Hello"** to your child!

How Long Does a Time-Out Need to Be?

Although a popular rule of thumb about how much time children need to be in time-out is one minute per year of their age, there is no one agreed-upon rule. *I believe the point is to get your child's attention and to remove yours.* The point is not for a child to be completely settled down before she can "get out" of a time-out, nor is it worthwhile to insist on an apology. "I'm sorry" may be the "right" thing to say, but it has little meaning in that context.

Since all parents have lots of things to do, I believe that spending about ten seconds or so is a reasonable time frame to be away from whatever needs doing. Kids may (and often do) decide that they need to carry on for more than the ten seconds, but the adults do not need to participate. There will be times and situations where it makes sense to be in time-out longer, but no adult attention need be given during that time.

3, Yes. Punishment, No.

"That's 3! Time-out." By including the number three in that phrase, the focus is away from the adult and is on the child's choice (without a lecture). No more talk is needed—not one word. Talking or looking at a child is giving attention. At "three," the goal is to remove adult attention.

Details

"No bowl in the sink. That's 3, time-out." *No more words* are needed. Take the child to a room or a place of your choice. As stated, I prefer a room with a door to prevent running-chasing-power struggle scenes. Close the door, or walk away or just turn away if it is a more open place, the point being to *remove attention*.

If the time-out location is a room, be ready for possible escape attempts, so holding the doorknob or adding a "toddler-proof" attachment to the inside doorknob or even a lock on the outside doorknob can be helpful.

The point of a time-out is *not to engage in a power struggle* over the location.

Count five seconds to yourself: no talk, no matter what, whether the child is silent, playing, laughing, crying, screaming, or throwing things. It has happened that a child might decide to pee. The removing adult attention no matter what rule includes even this sort of unsavory scene.

After about 5 seconds, open the door (beware of flying objects) and say, *brightly*, **"Are you all set with your time-out? Are you all set to put your bowl in the sink?"**

If there is a "Yes," a little nod, or *any sign* of settling, say, **"Great!!"** Give a big hug.

If the room has turned into a messy state during the time-out, it will need to be cleaned up before emerging. If a child wants adults to help, that's fine.

If the timed-out child is not ready, say only **"Oh, I see you're not ready,"** and repeat the time-out. Ask again if she is all set and ready to end the time-out.

Ending the Time-Out

After two rounds, you can end it by saying only, **"Time-out is all done. You may come out when you are ready. I'll be downstairs,"** and go about your business. Proceed directly to your next project or location.

Check in periodically on the Mr.-or-Ms.-who-is-deciding-to-stay-in-the-room-and-play (scream, laugh, go to sleep). Of course, if you suspect foul play, if your child is doing something unsafe or there is blood, a check-in is warranted; otherwise, from time to time, offer **"Are you all set to come out (downstairs, etc)? Are you ready to put the bowl in the sink?"** It is important that the adult *not* get into the trap of ordering your child to do the deed. It is important for your child to decide herself. Again, we are not interested in the focus of the 'problem' being in the wrong spot, on the adult. By the same token, I do not advise getting into the terrible trap of trying to teach a lesson.

When the timed-outer decides to be all set, the response will be, **"Oh, I'm so glad to see you!"**—warmly, even if you don't feel so warm. In this case, "warmly" does not refer to angrily. It refers to the nice kind of warm.

Some children will decide to keep their tantrums going; others may go to sleep, stay in the room for extended periods of time, or even come out and swing into cooperative behaviors—or the exact opposite.

> The value of giving children the chance to end their time-out adds to the spirit of giving them the power to make their own choices, thus avoiding the "adults-will-never-win" power struggles.

More About Location in the World of Time-Outs

If the ten-second (to start with) time-out method involves a room with a door, this is effective for children ages two to five, or whatever size is possible for you to easily carry a child to the time-out room. This depends on your health and the size of the child. It is not a good idea to transport a child anywhere if you are in danger of re-injuring a weak back or spraining a shoulder.

How Long? How Short?

Time spent in a time-out can always be increased; however, since the goal is to get the child's attention and be able to move on, it makes sense to try the shorter periods of time first. Kids can carry on tantrums for amazingly long periods of time. If kids need to have a tantrum, then that's what they need to do. An occasional checking in with them is encouraged, but only to tend to business. For example, **"Are you all done with your time-out?"** and **"Oh, good. All set to take the toys off the table?"** That's plenty of attention and words. If yes, great. If no, then the unhappy child is clearly not ready yet, but she may come out whenever she likes. Your contribution? **"I will be downstairs."** Period.

Getting the toys off the table (or the bowl in the sink, the teeth brushed, etc) and getting back to the business of having some fun is the goal. That's it. Nothing more, nothing less. Move on.

Removing Adult Attention Anywhere

Time-outs can be done without the availability of a room with a door by simply REMOVING ALL ATTENTION.

If the location is other than a room with the door, after giving counting clues and saying **"That's 3, time-out. No hitting,"** don't look, don't touch, don't say anything for about five seconds. No talking, even if the child is deciding to climb up your body or cling to your leg,. Then, as usual (brightly), **"Are you all**

done with your time-out?"

Wait for a response of some kind and then respond either **"Oh, you're not ready,"** and return to no attention, or "**Oh, good. I'm so glad. Are you ready to sit at the table now?"** Clearly, a time-out without a door may be less effective in removing attention. It is a clearer response when you are outside the door and the child is inside the door.

Taking a break, taking space, and stopping to think are implemented so that all the participants will have a chance to be less focused on further drama and difficulties.

While you are holding the doorknob, this can be considered luxury time, a time for willing yourself to think of.....a tropical paradise, your favorite ice cream, a massage. You get the picture. No matter what is going on loudly or softly behind the closed door, this can be a nice time for you. After all, a time-out is a time-out for everyone, a method of anger management for all ages.

If adult attention is not removed, parents fall into the trap of chaos, frustration, or forcing the child do something, which usually leaves adults in a shaky, tenuous position. So say only, **"That's 3, time-out."** Period. End of story. Short story. Ten seconds worth of story. Move on. Adults need to remain in as dignified a position as possible. Even if the time-out needs to be extended for a longer period of time, losing dignity is not advised, and by using these steps there is a better chance for adult success in this sensitive area.

Behind a closed door, it really shouldn't matter if a child in time-out is crying, screaming, laughing, playing, throwing things or saying hateful things directed at the all-suffering parent or to others near and far.

What matters is that the child has decided to get to the 3, either automatically or via counting clues. The focus need not be on the mean adult imposing a time-out or, for that matter, a work-off of a 3. The focus is on the sad events surrounding the child's choosing to get to the 3, but without blame and lectures.

"BUT I CHANGED MY MIND!"

A Cooperation Counts Mother of a Five-Year-Old writes:

"Tonight, before we got to the pizza store, I said that I would be watching for chances to give out stars for great restaurant behaviors. While waiting for our food, Tasha discovered the candy display and wanted some. I agreed, but told her that would mean no dessert. She got a package of gum. All was well until we got home, when she spotted the brownies on the counter. She spit her gum into the trash along with the rest of the package, and wanted brownies. I reminded her that dessert was all done for tonight. So, as you can imagine, she was *not* happy. What ensued was screaming, yelling, and stomping around.

I reminded her that she could be mad, but needed to go into the other room and be mad there. We had been practicing **"That's 3, take space"** and, without even needing to give any counting clues, she ran behind the couch and calmed herself down! I stayed cool as a cucumber and resisted the urge to give her a lecture about the evils of changing her mind, as I would have done before Cooperation Counts parenting strategies became a fixture in our house. A few minutes later, when she was quieter, we were able to discuss why she was so upset. I listened to her without saying anything other than asking her things like, "What happened next?" and "What was that like for you when you realized there would really be no more dessert?"

Soon *she* figured out that she had wanted the gum at the time but changed her mind when she saw the brownies. I agreed that the discovery of the brownies made her sad. She also told me she thought all of her stars would be taken away because of the way she'd behaved over the brownie problem. I thanked her for telling me what was worrying her and explained that all of the stars she earned always stayed and she had even earned one star for great behavior at the restaurant and another one for deciding to take space behind the couch when she had been so upset!. Two more stars went up, we hugged and did our fun star dance!

I know it won't always be easy to handle tough situations, but the approaches I use now make such good sense. A big bonus is the fact that I can stay calm, even if Tasha is involved in a scene! I don't need to panic anymore, and that helps everything!"

When the Time-Out is Done, It's Done. Head for Some Fun!

Making a conscious effort to move on is definitely the way to go. Staying stuck in negatives is not. Having fun is what being with each other is all about!

Take Space, Look for a Place

It is a joyful moment when our children decide to take space instead of revving up to a nasty scene. Stars are gladly given for such choices (Chapter 3). It is perfectly acceptable to identify a time-out as a take-space, and everyone, older and younger, can get creative in finding such places. Some have included behind a couch, under a table, the space between the desk and a chair, or a tent made of towels and blankets. March around the house looking for creative take-space places and head for the stars!

Reminder: If a Time-Out is Necessary, It Can be Effective Just by Removing Adult Attention- Respectfully

If taking space is not a reality, and there is no room with a door available, or if it is a parental decision not to use this location, time warnings, counting clues, or an automatic **"That's 3." Time-out. No throwing food,"** then other strategies are called for. Move Ms. Deciding-To-Throw-Food to another location, holding her away from you firmly and avoiding any conversation. Avert your eyes. No talking. In a few seconds, look at her and say, brightly, **"Are you all set? Are you all ready to go back to the table?"** If there is any (even a tiny) sign of a possible "Yes" or "OK"—no words are required or needed, show your pleasure. **"Great! Back to the table. Remember, no throwing food. All set?"** This can be repeated until you are tired or lose interest. Then, you can end the time-out by saying, **"All done. Let's go back to the table and try again."** Continue to remove any attention by turning your head and saying nothing except periodically, **"Are you all set to be with me nicely?"** If the answer is yes, or if there is even a nod, **"Great!"** If not, continue to remove "the audience" by no looking and no talking.

Time-Out Tips in Public

Once we have the basics in place, giving a time-out in public is not as difficult a concept as it may first appear. The basic principles apply. Removing a child from a store or a restaurant means giving time warnings, counting clues, and then—at **"That's 3, time-out"** comes the removal. Leaving a cart full of groceries, food on a table in a restaurant, or a special location of any sort, all can be done if a young child decides to get to the sad 3. Say **"That's 3, time-out"** as if the phrase were one word. Remember the very few words and counting clues option, which takes the bad-guy hat off the adult. Removing adult attention by not looking, talking, or touching (except, of course, to take the "That's 3" child from the area) is simple and effective. The removal can be outside the restaurant, into the car, or away from an area. The distance or amount of time is not as important as the fact that it has happened at all.

Adults Taking Time-Out: Conscious Disengagement

Conscious disengagement is very different from ignoring. **"I'm stopping to think. I'll get back to you in a minute"** is a handy phrase along with **"That's 3. I'm in time-out."** Don't look, don't talk, don't touch and then, a few seconds later, look at your child and say only, **"Are you all set to be with me nicely?"**

If trouble persists, say only, **"Oh, I see you're not ready for me to end my time-out,"** and back you go into the land of thoughtful, conscious disengagement. Repeat as needed for as long as you are interested in prolonging this particular scene. The age-old parenting tradition of taking an adult break is often wise. While some call it "anger management," I call it "survival." Of course, when counting clues are introduced, the instant message is that you are serious and that now is the end of lectures or nagging.

Consider that an adult time-out might be a good time to use parenting strategy #7,500. This number is only an estimate, as the number is really in the "unimaginably high" category. Try this: **"I am angry (disappointed, frustrated, upset) and I am going to take a break. I will get back to you shortly."** Actually change your location or just close your eyes, or turn in the other direction. There is no law that says an adult must have an answer for everything and at that precise moment. Besides, role-modeling how to stop, take a breath, and compose oneself are all good things for us to do, and it is wonderful for the kids to see some "heat of the moment" thoughtful choice possibilities. This may take some waiting it out while your not-so-quiet darling rages. He is just not ready to be with you quite yet.

Since no props of any kind are needed, these strategies can be used in virtually any location and under any circumstance. When parents have Cooperation Counts in place, there is a tendency to be able to think more clearly, and there is a better chance to put creative time-outs as well as other thoughtful parenting strategies in place.

About 3's and Stars Charts for the Younger Set

When are children old enough to have a real 3's chart with stated problems and work-offs? Parents will decide this on an individual basis, but typically, children between the ages of three and four are ready to head into the land of cause and effect via the Cooperation Counts methods. If an older sibling is using this system, the explanation of a 3's chart will be understood more quickly. In any case, a short explanation is in order. Very young children can have an immediate response to a 3 by using an effective time-out. They have also been known to do very well with the addition of 3's and stars charts and this plan quickly becomes a usual part of daily family life.

Remember, a time-out is just an immediate response to a 3. It is not a work-off.

Yes, both an effective time-out and a work-off of a 3 can happen. That's fine. But please don't confuse the two.

Giving Information With Only a Very Few Words

"Seatbelt on please." "It's almost time to put toys away." "No throwing food."

Parents as Cheerleaders

Many positive phrases can be used with even the youngest children. Here are a few, but the trick is to say them with ENTHUSIASM!

"Wow!!! Great taking space. You were so mad but you decided to settle down behind the couch. Wonderful!" (This can be said even if, by accident, a little one wanders or even stomps away.)

"YES!!! Great putting on your shirt!"

"WAY TO GO!!! Great picking up your toy!"

"THANK YOU for putting the book on the shelf!"

"YAY!!! I LOVE the way you wiped your nose."

Parents as Picture Painters

Using "visuals" can go a long way. How about putting a stop sign or even a big "3" on a forbidden item or location?

THE GREAT ESCAPE(S)

Involving the kids is always a plus. Even a child writing a note on a piece of paper stuck to a door can be an important reminder for everyone to "read."

Chad, age three, was an escape artist. He had gotten out of doors at night, and once that even happened in a snowstorm! He decided to stop being an escape artist only after his older brother (age four) put a "sign" (paper with some marks on it) on all of the doors, because, as he told his little brother, "I don't want you to go outside by yourself." Short of twenty-four-hour Chad duty, other efforts by this family to keep him inside had failed. They had even put locks on the doors and windows. Though Chad couldn't open them, he still woke everyone up by making noise as he tried to get those locks open. But his brother's "signs" did the trick! Chad decided to abandon his night-time lock-picking and illegal outside location. The family gratefully returned to their usual sleeping routine. The locks stayed on. The "signs" were up. Chad was in his bed. Visuals can be pretty powerful!

SUMMARY

Having a framework for discipline and praise applied in respectful, clear, move-on modes without lectures, threats or broken promises, can be the key to enjoying each other more of the time. That is everyone's goal. But parenting is more than just about 3's, work-offs, time-outs and stars; it is a constant journey towards finding our best selves. There are challenges every step of the way, and achieving the goal of relationships that can weather the inevitable storms is well worth it.

CHAPTER 6
WHAT IF MY CHILD HAS A DIAGNOSIS?

Every child and every family must have basic safety rules in order to survive. Even when a child has a diagnosis—for example, a learning disability, mood issues, an autism spectrum disorder, anxiety, or ADHD—parents need to be able to follow through with enforcing basic limits, especially if there is a challenging child in the mix.

Parents know their children best. They will not ask their children to do anything impossible for their age, size, personality or diagnosis. Asking a child to brush his teeth—if he is realistically capable of doing so—is a reasonable request, whether there is a diagnosis or not.

Keeping expectations in perspective is important. Work-offs are in the hands of the adults who have been able to calm down when it is time for that work-off. Depending on the diagnosis, the consequence, as well as the timing of it, is chosen to fit the situation.

Parental decisions must be made "in sickness and in health," and Cooperation Counts offers simple tools that can be used in every daily life scene regardless of diagnosis, situation or history. All relationships are complicated. Complicated relationships often lead to more complicated responses, but the same rules apply: Be consistent, be clear, follow through, and move on.

I have made the point earlier that there is a big difference between "Can't" and "Won't." This is true whether or not the child has a diagnosis, but parents must take the diagnosis into consideration when they decide how to discipline and praise. Generally, simple, clear, fair, predictable parental responses with very few words lead to appropriate interventions.

Family life continues in times of crisis or calm. When cool heads prevail, thoughtful problem-solving is more likely to occur.

Finding and having tools to address the challenges of everyday life with children—all children—is a necessity. Finding ways to have fun with our kids of all ages is an absolute must.

Special Circumstances

If a child has a long history of violent rages where injury is done to himself or others, property is destroyed, or there is violence towards others more than occasionally, it is advised to seek professional help.

It is possible that, in a thoughtful way, the tools of the Cooperation Counts system can be adapted. For instance, it has happened that the kids are the ones to choose their own consequences. This could be done to further remove the adult from the focus of anger when it is consequence time. If there are no consequences at all, additional chaos could ensue. By choosing their own consequences, consider the following: As an example, the consequence (work-off of a 3) could always be either losing one hour of Lego time, getting no dessert, or losing cell phone minutes. There have been some instances where the kids have chosen much more difficult consequences than their parents would ever consider. This could turn a lemon scene into lemonade for the parents. If the child chooses "no screens for the whole day," the parent could respond with **"That seems pretty tough. Let's consider no screens for two hours."**

These adaptations could be made in conjunction with a specialist, but if this is to happen only with parental input, adaptations can be considered thoughtfully and always with the option to reassess the plan.

NO, NO, NO!!!!
(Adapting the Tools)

Sarah was eight and Annie was ten. Annie had always been a "no" girl. This dismal situation was making everyone exhausted since "NO!" would often lead to big tantrums. To make things even more complicated, there was no predicting when she would change from sweet as pie to exactly the opposite—loudly! Everyone was worried, of course, and in their quest to find some solutions, they were referred to me through a psychiatrist who was helping with the assessment process. Neuropsychological testing was in the works as well, but then there was daily life, which continued to be severely disrupted. The experts and family agreed: There needed to be some changes at home.

The family quickly learned the Cooperation Counts program, and when it was firmly in place, parenting strategies were added along with appropriate adaptations of the basic system. Annie soon knew when her parents meant business. In addition, they were no longer in the "because I said so" mode. Power struggles were a snap to identify and avoid.

Take the socks scene. The rule was for Annie to put her dirty socks into the laundry basket. They hardly ever got there. This was a perfect "target behavior," which means that if it were to be turned around, her parents would be happy campers. It wasn't turned around. Actually, Annie seemed to dig her heels in even more, no pun intended. Annie's parents conferred and decided that it was not a life-or-death situation whether or not the dirty socks got into the laundry basket. The socks location was really about a power struggle set up by Ms. Annie. The reason was unknown.

Together, we decided to use the usual first portion of the Cooperation Counts tools—time warnings, **"Almost time,"** and **"Now it's time."** When Annie's parents got to **"Now it's time..."** they made a conscious decision. They saw the socks scene for what it really was: Annie could put them away if she decided to, but her usual choice was, "You can't make me." At **"Now it's time to put your socks in the laundry basket"** they sometimes decided not to add the counting clues as they realized that Annie would often decide to put the socks in the laundry basket when *she* decided to do so, and not before. Using the Cooperation Counts philosophy, her parents wanted to set her up for success, so they made a decision to let it go. After **"Now it's time...."** they would often say, **"I see you're not ready to put your socks in the basket right now,"** and that would be that. Everyone went about their business. The socks stayed in the same illegal location.

Ah—but remember that Annie had a younger sister? Sarah was very eager to accumulate her stars, and when Annie decided not to put those socks into the basket, guess who was happy to do so? Yes, sister Sarah! Soon, Annie got the idea that if she was interested in getting her own stars (which also equaled her parents smiling, giving high- five's, etc.) she could decide to get those nasty socks in the basket even faster than that silly Sarah. This turned into a win/win scene for all, and thoughtful parenting strategies prevailed.

WHAT IF A PARENT HAS A DIAGNOSIS?

Just as adaptations need to be made when a challenge presents itself in any area of our lives, it is best to problem-solve and look for solutions in thoughtful ways. This usually includes finding additional supports along the way.

Kayla's Story

Since adolescence, Kayla has been diagnosed with post traumatic stress and bipolar disorders. These have been challenging issues, to say the least. Now, as a wife, mother and step-mother in a blended family, she finds that her temper often gets the best of her and all of her relationships are rocky. There have been several formal separations. Everyone is upset and finds it difficult to manage the high level of stress, which is usually created by Kayla's unpredictable, intense moods.

When one of the children needed to be hospitalized as a result of uncontrollable tantrums and rages, my name was given to the family, and we began our work. For our first few appointments, Kayla was absent from the family as well as absent in our meetings. She was, literally, unable to function without rages and outbursts.

Fortunately, Kayla agreed to participate in a hospitalization, followed by a therapeutic day program. Medications were adjusted, and she returned to the family. She was calmer and eager to learn about the Cooperation Counts system, as she was longing to act in a more responsible manner. She rapidly embraced the system, which had been put into place during her absence. As a result, she quickly memorized the steps and scripts, was coached by everyone, and soon was taking her own time-outs when needed. We also decided that she was a great watcher-for-stars, and that her husband was best suited to be the "work-off guy," at least until Kayla was on firmer ground emotionally and because of the specifics of the family relationships.

Pretty soon, following the rules of using very few words, and getting out of power struggles via the time warnings and counting clues, the kids were making big efforts to gather their stars, which in itself helped undo the log jam of refusals. There was much less adult criticism and threats along with many fewer adult lectures. Everyone began to figure out ways to have fun together and proceeded to do so. The adults supported each other via the Cooperation Counts system tools. Red flags were easily identified and addressed within the family with minimal input needed from me. Best yet, Dad and the kids learned how to get out of Kayla's way instead of running right into her misery-making moods.

The family continues to live together much more happily. Discipline and loads of praise are in place. Adult tantrums happen in private, and everyone is problem-solving instead of being overwhelmed by the realistic challenges they all must face.

About Seeking Professional Help

The Cooperation Counts program is effective in coordination with ongoing treatment. Part of the beauty of the system is that it is easily adapted for therapists as well as for families. Behaviors do not exist in a vacuum. It is important to take into consideration a host of factors which might include issues of distractibility, frustration tolerance, mood, history, and patterns of concerning behaviors over time, to name only a few. Identifying red flags is vital, and one way to do that is to introduce a solid behavior management system. Just as combinations of natural supplements and Western medicines are often used in conjunction with therapeutic interventions, so it is that parenting strategies need to be looked at just as carefully. Whether there are diagnosed difficulties or not, all roads lead to the utilization of every resource available for the all-important task of raising our children.

CHAPTER 7

SAMPLE SCENES

ANGUISH IN THE AISLES

The Dreaded Atomic Meltdowns, At Home and In Public!

Elizabeth and Grace are four-year-old twins. Taking them any-where requires the patience of Job and sometimes even that is not good enough. Even at their tender ages, the kids have perfected the art of manipulation, divide and conquer, and defi-ance with a capital "D." These "accomplishments" have been the subject of many a conversation between their increasingly distressed parents. Money is tight. Except on very rare occa-sions, a babysitter is out, so real life includes taking Elizabeth and Grace to possible disaster locations, like stores. Use your imagination. Stores are perfect triggers for trouble. Children al-ways spot something that they must have—NOW—and if they don't get it...fill in the blanks. Elizabeth and Grace have been known to display BIG MELTDOWNS!

Super Size Store Stress

Before this family used the Cooperation Counts tools, people in many aisles could clearly hear Mom's voice. First, she sounded reasonable. Soon, reasonable turned to reasonable but firm. Firm was followed by annoyed. Begging and threats ensued. Mom got louder. Elizabeth and Grace got louder. Bribes were offered. Loudness prevailed. Needless to say, such scenes were extremely stressful for the adults. The jury is out about the younger set. Nevertheless, store situations were usually not serene.

By using the Cooperation Counts program, Mom now knew that she was no longer rendered helpless when the twins acted up. She was fair and clear. Guilt was gone. The girls were clear about the rules at each specific location which, with the store trip, included the exit from the house, the car, the parking lot, in the store, back into the car, and home.

Every Outing is a Training Mission

Mom embraced a fact of life. The trip to the store was not just a trip to the store; it was more of a training mission with an unknown beginning, middle, or end. Although getting the tuna fish for the longed for recipe was important, in terms of Cooperation

Counts philosophy, what was REALLY important was establishing a workable car, store, car, and home routine.

In order to set the girls up for success, Mom first made sure that the girls knew the rules of each step of their way. She followed with time warnings and then, wouldn't you know it, trouble started before they even left the front door. Elizabeth was fine with putting her jacket on. Grace was not! Mom, however, was now "equipped." There was no need for panic as in the past. She had a plan, whether or not the store outing happened and if even one child decided to make trouble. Mom knew that it was imperative that Grace and Elizabeth were deciding to cooperate, or the outing could not happen. Period.

Coat, No Coat

At this particular time, the tuna location remained a mystery. Whether it would be in the longed-for recipe or in the can on a distant shelf was as yet unknown. For now, the focus turned to Ms. Grace and her coat, which remained on the hall hook. The positive focus, however, went right to Elizabeth, whose coat was not only on her but was even zipped! The deciding-to-behave child was the focus of the first step, even though the non-cooperator remained dug in.

After praising Elizabeth and getting her settled with her dolls, Mom turned (brief) attention to Ms. No-Coat Grace by giving the time warnings. When it was clear that her choice was to continue to be coat-less, counting clues were given.

131

There was no arguing, begging, or threatening from Mom. There was only information with very few words, time warnings and counting clues.

Grace refused to put on her coat. Elizabeth continued to play with her dolls, receiving smiles and high-fives from Mom. Grace received only a few words in the form of counting clues and then **"That's 3. No coat. Time-out."** The Cooperation Counts style time-out was done (Chapter 5). No go. Grace was not ready to get the coat on. Maybe she didn't really even want to go to the store. Maybe she did. What was clear was the no-coat decision.

Uh Oh!

In the meantime, the scene took on a new dimension, as Elizabeth had about had it. Now, both children were stuck in an apparently escalating scene.

Mom was wise. She recorded the two 3's that Grace had decided to get on her chart and went to play with poor Elizabeth, announcing only that when both girls were settled down, ready to follow the rules, and if there was enough time, they could try again to find that tuna.

About 3's Charts for the Younger Ones

Some children at age four are ready for real 3's charts and work-offs. Some are only ready for the time-out tactic. This is a parental decision. Since Grace was in the "ready-for-3's-and-work-offs" category, two 3's went on her chart after the time-outs, with "No coat, store" on the problem line(s). The actual work-off(s) would be done at a later time when something was really important.

Sometimes opportunities come up where a work-off can connect with the problem. For example, another time, if Grace would like to go to a store with her Grandma and the answer could be "yes," the next step would be to **check her chart**. Uh oh. There are those Thursday 3's on her chart. The problems would be read aloud, **"No coat to go to the store on Thursday and no coat to go to the store on Thursday. Oh dear. The work-off is… no store with Grandma today."** This would be said sadly, kindly of course.

Another option for the work-off could be to wait for ten minutes to go to the store with Grandma, while Mom waited at home with Grace until the work-off was done. If Grace acted up, the time would need to be started over again. It was a good thing that this was a modern Grandma who had a cell phone! There was no problem locating her and Elizabeth when Grace's 3's were worked off.

Of course, during the ten minutes of waiting, if there was wailing or trouble of any sort in response to the sad work-off, there could be all sorts of empathy headed her way, but the time would still need to start over. Even if it turned out that there was no store adventure that day—not any—punishment would be replaced by a consequence, sympathetically done.

Hope Springs Eternal!

Let's say that Grace decided to put on her coat after her time-out(s). Wonderful! Off she goes!

The rules are again stated and Grace and Elizabeth both need to cooperate, or it is not only back to basics but most likely back to the house or car to try again. Setting up the kids for success is the goal—not pestering the one who is not cooperating. If both girls decide not to be ready, the same applies and Mom can go about her business, giving no attention to the refuser(s) until the scene is peaceful.

Focus on the One Who is Deciding to Behave

It makes sense to focus on the one who is deciding to behave. Counting clues are used quickly if there is trouble. "Nip-It-In-The-Bud" mode is in full swing.

If both Grace and Elizabeth have decided to be in their coats and seat belts, Mom can give them a cheer, clap for them, and be amazed at their choices.

When (if) the store trip moves along, lavish praise is given: **"I** loved the way you put the oranges in the bag."

Using these steps, Mom is not interested in being the boss. She is informational, respectful, and upbeat. She is looking for star choices as well as effectively managing the trouble spots.

Let's say that, finally, the little group gets to the grocery store, is in sight of the longed for (by Mom) tuna, and one of the kids decides that putting the oranges in the bag is no longer a fun game and.....trouble ensues!

Mom knows just what to do. Conversation can be offered but if that is not helping, time warnings, quick counting clues, a time-out in the form of turning her head, no talk, "all set," etc. and if the "trouble" one or ones continue, there is a plan. Abandon ship—meaning abandon the cart, and head for the car. This will either turn into a "take-space" time or the end of the store excursion.

Easy Come, Easy Go

What about the suddenly abandoned cart? Yes, it's true: Whole carts, even with frozen food in them, have been known to be left melting while kids and their Mom troop out of the store. The store manager may or may not have an opinion about this, but Mom has her priorities; the ethics of her decision can be debated later. It is a sad scene indeed—for the Mom. It also might be a sad scene for the kids later when they want popsicles and even more sadly, the popsicles are not in their house; they are in the cart at the store, completely melted. I'm sure that the child who did not decide to get the 3 that led to the premature good-bye to the popsicles will be offered something else. Even the timer-outer will be offered something nice. It just won't be (more sadness) the popsicle. Oh dear. There will be another day to try the store scene again, but there will not be any lectures.

Even if Grace and/or Elizabeth decide to take months to accomplish a successful store outing, the good news is that their Mom at least has a reasonable, predictable, consistent plan that replaces helplessness and hand wringing.

She might even decide to take only one child at a time to the store as **"it's just not working"** for the girls to be together. With the no-babysitter reality, these trips with only one child may be few and far between, but, after all, training takes time.

The kids will decide whether or not to put coats on, get buckled in car seats and stay that way, hold Mom's hand in the parking lot, stay in the cart, and so on. But for sure, there will be great joy whenever the outing happens successfully!

BEDTIME BLUES PART I: GOOD-NIGHT

Some parents get up in the morning dreading what the night will bring in the bedtime department. Since we already know that whether or not the child will go to sleep without a fuss is literally out of parental control, the worrying often begins many hours before the sun sets. There are many well-known strategies to manage this most challenging of times with children of all ages.

Back to Bed

One of those strategies has been addressed in the popular TV show "Super Nanny." Jo Frost shares her "Back to Bed" technique frequently. The system is clear and is suggested for even very young children. Basically, the first time a child gets out of bed, the adult gently and firmly leads her back to bed saying only "It's time for bed, darling." The second time the child comes out, the adult leads her back saying only "Bed." The next time—and all other times—the adult leads her back to bed saying nothing. This technique seems to make a lot of sense. I would add that it would be important to share the specifics of the plan with the child first. I would even go so far as to suggest some role-playing and showing clearly on a calendar which night the Back-to-Bed plan will begin. Only then, I suggest, should it be implemented.

Adults, of course, need to do some planning until there is more peace in the night. In addition, it helps when Cooperation Counts is in place first, because the adults will already have the kids' attention—an invaluable part of parenting. Then, counting clues can be given for returning to the room and being quiet. The "being quiet" part can get tricky. Ignoring a crying child is difficult, but very important. Most of us will tend to get brave when there is sleep or lack of it at stake.

As always, no more than two sets of counting clues should be given, since if a child's choice is to get two 3's in a row, this signifies a power struggle, which will most likely not be won by the adult. These are nasty and will not have a satisfactory ending, so it is better to avoid going there in the first place.

Of course, staying in one's room quietly all night is cause for celebration, joy, high-fives and an all-important star-maybe even a double one!

I believe that if a child chooses not go to sleep, that's up to her. I am also not particularly concerned about her location. I would not be happy on the floor, but most kids simply do not care.

I also believe, however, that even if a child has decided to stay up all night—or for large parts of it, her getting up and going to school routine will remain the same. Parents might choose to share the "sleepless night" information with teachers. This seems only fair, as it is likely that the refusing or "just-couldn't-get-to-sleep" child will be grumpy. Perhaps very grumpy.

All human beings must fall asleep eventually. But nodding off for a nap, under these circumstances, is in the illegal category and should be avoided.

The next night, the request is the same—for the child to be in her room and quiet so that others can sleep. Consistency, which includes a bedtime routine for kids of all ages, is a good thing. Time warnings, **"Now it's time…."** a last hug or a **"Good-night"**….and that's it. Two sets of counting clues can be given and the back-to-bed routine can be repeated for as long as necessary. It would even be OK for an exhausted parent to bring in additional back up, otherwise known as a friend, neighbor, or relative. These additional bodies are used as supports and can come in very handy. Doing a favor for a neighbor in exchange for back-up should certainly be considered.

Adults enjoy their quiet evenings and should have them regularly.

Handing out morning stars is gratifying for all ages!

BEDTIME BLUES PART 2: GOOD-NIGHT

Sasha, age 7, had frequent and intense tantrums, was diagnosed with sensory issues and poor appetite affecting his weight, and had a trauma history prior to his adoption at age two. For years, his parents were sleep deprived, which was having an impact on their health. While the family continued to work with other specialists, we rolled up our sleeves and addressed behavioral issues via establishing a clear framework for discipline and praise with the Cooperation Counts program, and added various parenting strategies. Once Sasha knew when his parents meant business and when they did not, we decided to address the problem of the distinctly non-peaceful nights.

Sasha's parents had made valiant attempts in the past to help their noisy-in-the-night son to stay in his own room, but with little success. He had nightmares about spiders, was ravenously hungry or hot or cold, and hated his bed. In truth, his exhausted

parents felt guilty if they did not comfort him whenever requested. They felt sorry for him and knew that being alone in the
night was likely to be a terrifying time for their son. They just
didn't know what to do, and Sasha knew that.

The difference this time, we all agree, was that the Cooperation Counts tools were solidly in place. Sasha's parents were
confident, clear, respectful, and followed through with time
warnings, counting clues, 3's, work-offs and stars. They used
very few words when they meant business. Actually, Sasha's
tantrums had decreased significantly. He was accepting the fact
that a work-off was a work-off, it was not negotiable, and when
it was done, it was done. Tantrums had no audience partici-
pation. Now, Sasha was accumulating stars at a dizzying rate.
Reading his star chart was a joy: "Ate a whole carrot"; "Took
space and got mad under the table instead of at Mom"; "No hitting anybody all morning/ all afternoon/ all day"; "Used words
to describe what happened to the toy," "Came in nicely from
playing outside," "Shared the sandcastle bucket with his friend."
Sasha even got stars for settling down quickly from a tantrum...
but....there was the night problem, and everybody except Sasha,
of course, was exhausted.

Night

Sasha's mother wrote about one night's experience as we
marched forward courageously.

"In the past I read to him in our room and then moved him to his own bed. This was not a good precedent. Last night I limited the reading time in our room to make sure he would have all his falling asleep cycle in his own room, without physical contact with me. I also told him earlier that by Wednesday the reading would be entirely in his room. He wanted to stay and cuddle in our room, but I wouldn't. Earlier I told him our cuddle time would be earlier in the day in the living room. I don't want to have the break from contact in one of our rooms because I think it puts him into a cycle of needing me in the night when he wakes. Soon, we were doing the reading and all of the falling asleep in his room so he could fully settle himself.

Since Sasha remembered (real) hunger and would often feel hungry in the night, some snacks were set out on his bedside table to be eaten whenever he chose to do so.

After reading and our good-night routine, Sasha asked to sleep in our room until Dad came in. I stayed firm and quietly took him back. Then he asked to move his cot. Again I moved him back. He had a short tantrum and again I moved him back. Then he was frustrated by his stuffy nose and again, I took him back. I didn't say a word. I just took him back.

After four to five times of taking him back, he stayed in his room and slept through the night! He didn't get as many hours of actual sleep last night because it took him longer to get to sleep, but we had zero interruptions in the middle of the night, which enabled deep sleep. I was even able to have quite a few peaceful dreams myself!

He ate a good breakfast, handled the often difficult routine of changing clothes and tooth brushing well, and we were ready for the day!"

Morning

Sasha now has quite an array of night stars and morning stars. I think his Mom deserves them, too. She says her reward is feeling healthier, since she has been getting more sleep herself. Now she is more able to help her son face difficult challenges successfully. Wonderful!

REBECCA RULES—OR SO SHE THINKS

Rebecca, age thirteen, is an only child. She behaves quite well everywhere except at home where, for many of those years, she has been creating loud objections whenever something does not go her way.

Her parents know that they have, in a very real sense, "trained" her to be in Princess mode. They have consulted numerous experts about how to change things, all to no avail. Their house looks like a library, with a whole section addressing the complicated subject of parenting. They have read the books, highlighted important sections and followed the advice exactly as written. Nothing has changed.

Fireworks

Home may be peaceful until the answer from the parents approaches anything like "We'll see," "Maybe later," or "Not now." The slightest thing can get the fireworks going, and Rebecca rapidly heats up. Her non-princess performances effectively increase the volume in their home environment, and she rages long and loud while her parents get more and more upset.

Rebecca's parents feel—and are—helpless. They are embarrassed at home and in public. They walk on egg shells, so to speak, and do everything they can to avoid the outbursts that they know will come when things don't go Rebecca's way.

The adults are constantly outraged and their marriage is in trouble. As Rebecca behaves in a more and more entitled manner, her parents become more and more exhausted.

They consult the experts again. They re-read their library of parenting books. Mom has a therapist. Rebecca has a therapist. Dad is not interested. Rebecca remains in Princess mode—LOUDLY! Her parents remain in Exasperated mode—LOUDLY!

When Rebecca's parents decided to use the Cooperation Counts program, they found that they were no longer yelling and nagging. Rebecca could no longer get her parents' attention when she was raging. If Rebecca decided that she would continue to be rude, refuse to clean up her messes, or continue to order her parents around like, "Make me my breakfast," it got her nowhere.

She tried desperately to wear her parents down. She wanted what she wanted and she would get it no matter what it took. Rebecca was furious when her parents made a request—very reasonable ones, I might add—and instead of getting them to react, they only gave counting clues or took their own space. Rebecca knew very quickly that when her parents said, **"That's one,"** it meant that they were serious and that it was up to her to decide to cooperate or not. That's it. Adult lectures, begging, bribing, and threats were replaced with time warnings and counting clues. This was not always easy for Rebecca's parents, but it was much better than raging arguments.

Rebecca was being given the power she had wanted all along—to make choices. If she decided to make positive choices, her wonderful world continued. If she decided to make poor choices, the work-offs were very sad for her. The good news was that everyone was able to move on, even when she decided "I don't care if I get 3's or not. I don't care about work-offs!

You can't make me care!"

And Rebecca was right. When using the Cooperation Counts system, her parents realized that "I don't care" is a trap and should be of no interest to them. None. There was no conversation about "trap" topics. It was simply not worth sapping precious energy that would surely be needed at other times.

Reflections

Nobody can make a child do something they do not want to do. They are in charge of their bodies and their brains. Emotions and other complications will emerge, of course, but when the dust settles, Rebecca can decide whether or not to accept her parents' wishes.

Rebecca's parents now know that if she decides to make a poor choice, it is just that—a poor choice.

Rebecca's Choice is not a Reflection of Their Parenting

It would only become a reflection of their parenting if they had continued with lectures, giving in, punishing, and all the other "solutions" they had previously used.

Simplicity

Keeping complicated situations complicated is not necessary. The simplicity of time warnings, counting clues, work-offs and stars makes more sense. Refusals (both silent and loud), defiance, and tantrums can be addressed simply and respectfully by following the program. When Rebecca's parents make a request and follow the Cooperation Counts rules, they are following through with ordinary safe limits, but minus the punishment element. When Rebecca decides to make positive choices, her daily life will reflect the fact that she has parents who can and will show their love and support for her as a person. When she makes poor choices, her parents will be able to stay in that same mode, even if her rages lead to the pollution of her immediate environment.

Emotions are a part of the fabric of who we are as people no matter what our age, stage or situation. The Cooperation Counts program ensures that adults act in respectful ways, especially when the kids are deciding not to cooperate.

THE FOOT AND THE REFRIGERATOR

It always happens. When Andrew is mad, he heads for the kitchen and his foot collides with the refrigerator door—hard! Andrew knows that this puts his parents over the top. He gets their attention all right!

Here we go again. Power struggles galore. "Don't you dare kick that refrigerator door!"

The door gets kicked (no surprise here). "I can't help it!" screams Andrew, age fifteen. "Yes you can!" roars his Dad. This sort of scene is enough to raise the blood pressure of most adults.

The Old Way

The old way of handling this undignified scene might include something like, "That's it! You kick that door one more time and you're losing your D.S. for two weeks and I mean it! This is outrageous. You are wrecking our Saturday and you did it last weekend, too. Your little brother has more sense than you do!"

Nothing about this adult outburst is OK. Intellectually, most parents know that, but emotions often get in the way. Shouting ensues and increases because frustration has set in. Frustration has set in because Andrew will not cooperate with the very reasonable request to maintain distance between his foot and the fridge. He doesn't have to kick it if he decides not to, but he kicks it, quite vigorously and most definitely on purpose. More frustration. More shouting. This scene is going nowhere, fast.

The Cooperation Counts Way

Dad: **"Andrew, I can see that you are furious with your sister! I remember yesterday when you were over the top and I saw you march right into your room to take some space. That was great."**

Andrew: "That was yesterday. Today is today. She makes me so mad I could kick twelve refrigerator doors. She's the one who should be taking space—not me! It's not my fault. You always blame me for everything. You treat me like a little kid. I'm sick and tired of it!" Another kick ensues.

There are many options for parental responses at this point, and the Cooperation Counts program is one of them. If it is chosen, it might sound like this:

Dad: **"Andrew, now it's time to stop kicking the refrigerator door."** As soon as he says **"Now it's time...."** there will be no more discussion from Dad. This is not one of those times to give a time warning.

Andrew decides to give another kick.

Dad: **"Andrew, that's one. No kicking."** Dad is refusing to get into this power struggle, and the decision is now Andrew's to make. Yes, there are emotions going on for both, but this is not the time to discuss them. For older kids, "That's one" could change to "First reminder." This is a parental choice.

As usual Andrew decides to continue kicking. Dad does not participate in any conversation other than to say, **"That's two. No kicking."** Andrew decides to kick again.

Dad: **"That's 3."** The 3 will go on Andrew's chart or anything handy that could be used as a chart. This scene is not about Dad, it is about Andrew's choices. In the "Problem" line will be written "Kicked fridge door."

Dad can give one more set of counting clues—but only one more set, since if Andrew decides to get a second 3, his father should stop any additional counting as a power struggle is now clearly in the mix. There will be two 3's on the chart. Andrew will be informed about the work-offs at the time that they happen. Dad is not interested in punishments or inflicting agony on Andrew, who has just made a poor choice. That's it. Relationships and behaviors are complicated, but using the system tools is simple and effective.

Maybe Andrew will decide to keep kicking the fridge. If he does, it is advised that he will get no further attention. Dad will go about his business, leaving Andrew to kick in peace. Removing attention is vital.

Damage Details

If there is damage to the refrigerator, the cost of the repair could go on Andrew's "bill." Since he has no job or steady income, he will need to pay it off by, for example, delaying the purchase of a new shirt he might want.

In any parent/child/teen scene there is the big picture and the little picture. In this situation, Andrew's decision to kick the door on Tuesday afternoon is the little picture. There will be thousands of other Tuesdays where the rule will be the same: "If you're mad, don't hurt anybody or anything." In the little picture, the refrigerator door may continue to be kicked by an angry Andrew. In the big and little pictures, if Andrew continues the illegal activity of kicking property, there will be work-offs. Deciding to kick, or not, is up to him.

If Andrew decides to cooperate by one or by two, he is "golden" even if he yells, "This is so stupid!" Even if he does the big stomp and eye rolling routine, Dad could either just thank him for ceasing the kicking or say nothing at all. Dad is encouraged to *focus on one behavior at a time*, and in this scene, it is the

151

kicking of the refrigerator door. The focus is not on the stomp-ing or the eye rolling. There are two 3's on the 3's chart. Period. They will be worked off sometime. End of story, for now.

The next day Andrew's friend invites him to go to the mall. If the answer could be "yes," Dad can encourage preparation for the mall adventure. Then, he would likely say, **"Let's check your chart"** in a calm, informational tone.

Viewing the Chart

"Oh no! I see two 3's: kicking the refrigerator door yesterday afternoon and kicking the refrigerator door again." Dad paus-es, thinks a little bit and then says, **"The work-off is...waiting for thirty minutes to go to the mall.... and the time starts when you're settled down."** He will not say "You can't go to the mall." He will say only, **"The work-off is waiting for thirty minutes."** No bad-guy hat here! Dad also needs to be empathetic about the work-off and cheer Andrew on. **"Great. The time can start now."** Soon, **"Only eighteen minutes left to go!"**

Reminder: A work-off is a consequence. A consequence has two components: 1) It is something important and 2) It will—or won't happen—no matter what Andrew says or does. In this instance, it is very important to go to the mall, and he cannot get there without a car and a driver. Even if Andrew says he doesn't care, let's keep in mind we know for a fact that he does.

The next day, Andrew is MAD! His foot connects with the fridge. He will be given counting clues by a calm Dad, and Andrew will decide about whether not to continue the kicking.

Simple strategies can definitely effectively address complex circumstances.

THE LAUNDRY LESSON

It happens a lot. Kids of all ages accumulate humongous piles of laundry. These incredible piles are usually of great interest to parents but of little or no interest to their owners. Thinking philosophically is great but…what to do about the mess?

This is how one Cooperation Counts family decided to handle the impasse:

Rachel, age fourteen, owned a very nice laundry basket. She had actually picked it out herself and once upon a time it was deemed "perfect!" The agreed-upon deal was that clothes needing to be washed would appear downstairs, in the basket, and Mom would take care of them from there. The basket hardly ever appeared in the downstairs location.

After a lot of Grumbling (notice the capital letter "G") by both Mom and Rachel, Mom decided she would get herself right out of this no-win power struggle. The first step was accomplished by clearly identifying the problem: Rachel could either do her own laundry or bring it downstairs for her Mom to do. Mom's second step was to decide what to do—or not do—about the situation, which was of high interest to her but clearly not to Rachel. Mom thoughtfully put together a plan. There are three powerful words here—"power" "struggle" and "thoughtfully."

First, Mom made sure that the Cooperation Counts system was clearly in place. Rachel now knew when Mom was serious. Rachel also knew that there would be no begging, bribing, nagging, empty threats, criticism or displays of outrage by Mom.

The Problem, The Solution

Mom stated the problem clearly and then asked Rachel how long she would need to get her laundry together and downstairs. They agreed that by the next day at 5:00 if it was not downstairs, Mom would be off the hook. The laundry would not get done by Mom until Rachel decided to follow the in-place rule, which was to bring it downstairs. Period. No counting clues, but a boundary/time limit was in place. There would be follow through by Mom, but Rachel would be in the driver's seat about her own choice.

Less is Best

Rachel was given time warnings about the deadline, but by 5:00, her wash was not downstairs. Mom did nothing. She said nothing. She had lots to do and she went about the business of doing it. Inside, though, she was not particularly calm. Among other things, she envisioned Rachel going to school in dirty clothes.

Somehow Rachel managed to handle the situation. Mom somehow managed to hold the line of doing nothing and saying nothing—even when Rachel's piles got even bigger in her room. Yay for Mom! She refused to get into the power struggle and in the process, maintained her dignity.

Follow-through, minus lessons and lecturing, was alive and well. Mom insisted on enjoying Rachel. She did not even bring up the subject of the laundry. That would have been a waste of energy, and Mom was not interested.

After about a month, one day she noticed that Rachel was doing some laundry on her own! Mom resisted the urge to say anything like, "You finally decided to get going on your laundry, huh?" or "I see you finally came to your senses about your wash." or "Wouldn't it have been easier to just either give the basket to me or even do it yourself a long time ago?" Mom said nothing except to compliment Rachel on her positive choice and made sure that she had the washing and drying supplies she needed. There had been no arguing about the laundry. Smart Mom!

CHAPTER 8

USING COOPERATION COUNTS STEPS: A PRACTICAL GUIDE TO EVERYDAY TROUBLES

> *Child:* **"I'm NOT talking back. My Mom's being mean. I just want to watch TV."**
>
> *Mom:* **"It's not my fault that I sound so frustrated. I am! You're so rude! Every time I say it's time to turn off the TV, I get the same attitude! "**

This is only one example of trouble in everyday family life. The following steps can be applied whenever the kids make poor choices.

Ban the Word 'Bad'

Banning the word 'bad' is strongly advised. It does no good and can actually do harm. The phrase 'poor choice' can be easily substituted.

When there is trouble—refusal, defiance, etc.—is not the time to debate about who is right and who is wrong. Usually, it is best for adults never to take a side, as this leads them straight into a probable trap. In addition, pointless debates deplete adult energy, while kids seem to have endless energy for anything they are passionate about. Adults tend to get worn down more easily, which can lead to even more trouble. When there is an adult-child disagreement, it is unlikely that an acceptable resolution is in the cards. The idea that there is a resolution acceptable to all tends to be magical thinking. Magical thinking doesn't usually have a place in everyday life. Using the Cooperation Counts steps can be a reasonable option. Adults have a clear plan about avoiding tricky traps and purposeless power struggles. "You will!" "I won't!" and "You can't make me!" is a frequent dialogue, but it can only occur if the adults allow it. As previously stated, there is a big difference between a conversation and an argument, and it is unrealistic to expect that the kids will do something positive about it. Empathy in the form of understanding—really understanding—that a child's wish to keep the TV on is fine, as long as there is a conversation in which the parent recognizes the sadness of turning it off. Cooperation Counts system tools avoid arguments.

Real Life Responses, Cooperation Counts Style

State the problem: **"It's hard to end TV time."**

Using Cooperation Counts steps, give time warnings and counting clues when the adult is serious. There is no rule that says if one person says something, the other needs to respond in any specific way. I suggest that if there is conversation about the sadness of the imminent end of TV time, fine. If the conversation turns into an argument or rudeness, stop responding except to say, **"In four minutes it will be time to turn off the TV."** That's it. Nothing else. The TV may or may not get turned off.

Go about your business or, if there is not an argument, consider consoling the unhappy child who is in a potential panic at the very thought of the TV being in the off position. But consoling is only suggested if the tone is conversational. You will know the signs of an imminent argument. Don't go there. Resist the urge to participate in a no-win argument. The truth is that adult back-talk is as ineffective as child back-talk.

When you say, **"The TV goes off in three minutes,"** this has nothing to do with "because I said so." You are being fair and respectful—the best attitude for a parent to take.

The request for the TV to be shut off is not an impossible one. The kids can turn it off if they decide to do so. They may not want to, but they can. Remember, parents are not asking for the answer to a calculus problem to be produced in five minutes. The request is merely to turn off the TV. It may not be a popular request but parenting is not a popularity contest.

Let Go of the Lectures

This is not the time to give a lecture on how kids' brains may not develop properly or how their social skills will be forever affected if they watch too much TV. Kids can do a superb job of paying no attention to words they do not want to hear.

Continue With Time Warnings

Say only **"In two minutes it will be time to turn off the TV."** It often happens that at a one- or two-minute warning, kids have been known to object in a variety of tones and scenes. Responses are varied and can range from jumping up to turn off the TV right away, to crying (quietly or loudly), pleading, screaming, negotiating (often in ingenious ways), and rolling their eyes. These are not unusual responses, and kids do try to throw their parents off-track in a variety of ways. Do not be fooled. These are traps. They do not warrant attention or energy other than, perhaps, **"Thank you for letting me know."**

Traps

"I don't care if I get a 3!"
"I won't turn it off no matter what you say."
"I hate you! You never understand what I want."

"You never let me do anything!"

"You're just mad at me because I accidentally spilled the spaghetti on the new carpet."

"You're so mean!"

"I promise I'll clean up my entire room perfectly if I can only watch TV until ..." and more.

Stay on Track With Time Warnings and Counting Clues

Avoid getting caught in traps. Avoid saying anything or doing anything, except to stay on track: **"In one minute it will be time to turn off the TV."** Remember: It is best not to anticipate the outcome and to consciously work at not taking the outcome personally.

Say only, **"Now it's time to turn off the TV"** and proceed with the Cooperation Counts style counting clues steps (Chapter 1).

Focus on One Behavior at a Time

If the TV gets turned off and there is stomping, mumbling, or more than mumbling, say only **"Thank you."** Nothing more. Focus on one behavior at a time. Of course, rudeness is not the best response, but staying focused on the TV being off or on allows for a chance to avoid a major train wreck.

When a predictable framework of discipline and praise is in

place, parents can relax enough to consciously address the complicated business of thoughtful parenting.

THOUGHTFUL PARENTING TIPS

Look Into the Mirror
Let's make sure the messages we want to give are the ones actually given. Check your expression. What do you really look like to others?

Clapping and Cheering
Not only are clapping and cheering advised, but adding enthusiastic high-five's, hug and handshakes are encouraged as well.

"I'll Get Back to You About That."
Stepping away from the fray, never making a decision in the heat of the moment and taking some time to settle down, all increase the possibility of thoughtful decisions.

Give Information, Not Lectures
"The car will be leaving in ten minutes."
"I will consider that carefully and let you know."

Parents cannot always decide how to respond in the blink of an eye. It usually takes longer than that.

Triggers to the Troubles

Using the Cooperation Counts program helps to identify specifics as well as patterns that lead to positive or poor choices and encourages parents to identify and work with possible roadblocks. When adults are aware of specific triggers, they can address them thoughtfully.

Setting the Kids Up for Success

Consider this: If a toddler is headed straight for a carefully constructed Lego project, rather than berating the engineer of the masterpiece for yelling at the intruder, how about just removing the "trouble"? That would be the toddler. Construction continues!

Setting the Adults Up for Success

Just as parent/child relationships are complicated, so it is with adult/adult relationships. Wish lists can be wonderful. If this or that could be changed, what would it be? One idea: pick one as a goal, give it a try, and then reassess if that has helped. For example, it often happens that the adult who is at home the most will call the other frequently. These calls are not always filled with sweetness and light. They are often the complaining type of calls, usually having to do with trouble with the kids. Cooperation Counts parents often find that these unhappy calls become much less frequent as the power struggles at home diminish.

CREATIVE WAYS TO TRACK 3'S AND STARS

One goal for Cooperation Counts adults is to use as little energy as possible when there is trouble in the parenting department. The use of technology, as it turns out, can help in this effort.

Cameras and Computers

Photos can be visible ways of keeping track of all sorts of important things. They can also be downloaded onto computers. Keeping track of 3's, work-offs, and stars becomes an easy job, even if a 3's chart mysteriously disappears or is discovered in shreds at the bottom of the trash can, or even if its whereabouts are never known!

The Blackberry Scene

Dan is the father of three lively girls. He also happens to own a Blackberry. The driving-to-school scene is especially nerve-wracking for him.

Cooperation Counts is clearly in place at home. Now, whenever there is trouble in the car—or anywhere else—he doesn't need to give many counting clues. He just reaches for his Blackberry and the kids know that he is getting ready to keep track of any car 3's. Getting his Blackberry into position can also mean he will track the stars. That's up to the kids!

Keeping Track The Old Fashioned Way

Keep a small notebook in the parental pocket. Jot down information that can be addressed as you go along with your day and translate the information to the home chart. Multiple children can each have a section in the book. Each child's section can even be color coded with different colored paper clips or tabs.

The Beauty of a Binder

A 3's and stars chart for each child can be added to a binder. This way, the charts can be visible but also kept safely away from mystery disappearances and even occasional crumpling.

You've Got Mail

Email or text material to yourself as a reminder and transfer information to the home chart promptly.

The Family as a Team: Kids Watching for Stars

Just as adults are encouraged to catch the kids making good choices, so each child as a family team member can be encouraged to catch his parents and siblings doing something wonderful. This is a whole lot easier to take than tattle-tailing and complaining about each other!

Having fun is at the very top of the "Job Description for Parents." Insist on it.

CHAPTER 9
ANGER MANAGEMENT FOR ALL AGES: TAKING A CALM BREAK IN TIMES OF TROUBLE

As I have stated earlier, the Cooperation Counts program actually turns out to be an anger management program for everyone. The goal is to be able to handle the non-joyous times with some measure of dignity and to move on as quickly as possible. After buttons are pushed, this goal is often elusive, but with the tools of the program, the "quickly" part is in full swing.

Most adults know, at least intellectually, that it is never a good idea to solve a problem while in the heat of a difficult moment. Don't take unkind, angry words from kids personally. Using the Cooperation Counts system instantly gives tools for everyone to take a break from the troubles. Choices are given.

Adults do not need to base the success of their parenting on children making great choices.

Working Off 3's in Cooled-Down Mode

When there is a work-off of a 3, adults have a chance to be in a cooled-down frame of mind. Time, even a little, has passed since the emotion of the miserable moments. At the time of a work-off, adults have a better chance to be more reasonable rather than raging, and are therefore in a better position to re-fuse the punisher role.

> Using the Cooperation Counts steps, there is consistent follow through—minus anger, criticism, and shame. This is a big deal in the world of parenting.

Later, in a quieter moment after the "storm," you might say: **"I was thinking about this morning when it was time to turn off the TV. You were so upset. Do you want to tell me about it?"**

Tell Me More

Whatever the response, go with the flow. For example **"Tell me more"** is a wonderful response. Just listen and say very little. Additional phrases could be: **"What happened next?" "What** was that like for you?" "Really?" "Oh, I see." These simple and well known phrases turn out to be powerful tools for improving complicated relationships.

Stepping Back

The Cooperation Counts program provides a clear plan whereby the adults as well as the kids can look at their own behaviors, choices, and responses within the safety of an easy system that makes sense. Under ordinary circumstances, anger levels and defensiveness tend to be raised. But with the Cooperation Counts system, everyone can step back when counting clues begin, leaving time and energy for making more thoughtful choices. This is a gift in the parenting department, and who doesn't welcome such a gift?

When the Kids Just Won't Take Space

When older kids just won't take space, and since power struggles are out, adults can take their own space/time-out/break/ mellow moments. Time warnings and counting clues can either be given or not. That is up to the adults, but a response to a three could be **"That's 3. I'm taking my break."** This can be done while remaining with your child or teen. No talk, no touching, no looking other than, **"Are you all set to be with me nicely?"** No lectures or lessons are necessary. If we look for something like "Mom, I'm SO sorry that I wouldn't shut the cabinet door," this probably won't happen, at least not in the heat of the moment, and isn't important, anyway. Removing the audience is what is important.

Being Older Can be a Good Thing

"I hear rude talk. It's just not working out for us right now. I'm going to take a break and do an errand." It can actually be a blessing when kids are old enough to be left alone for a few minutes. While you are out, answer the cell phone or a text only if you choose to do so and the tone, verbal or written, is acceptable. Always leave emergency information in a visible spot to be used when a parent cannot be reached. Call, text, or return and say only, **"Are you ready to be with me pleasantly?"**

Another option is to say nothing at all to Mr. or Ms. Rude Talk. If the coast appears to be clear, refuse to be lured into any traps that could lead into more trouble, and move on. Resist the urge to teach a lesson. This is not impossible. It can be done.

Being the Target of Anger
and What Happens Then?

Children and adults of all ages are not equipped by nature to withstand barrages of anger directed toward them, and anger management is a tough task for everyone. In the parenting department, it is vital to find ways to avoid destructive negatives as the outlet to manage our own frustrations. It is unhealthy for everyone, but the "management" part of anger presents real challenges that must be addressed in order to prevent harm to our children's positive sense of themselves.

Rising Rage

Finding and using a daily life parenting system to manage mounting adult rage is a must. If it isn't the Cooperation Counts program, any system that includes parents using kind, thoughtful, respectful, clear, firm ways, especially when the kids are acting up, is essential.

If a child were to be placed in a classroom where the teacher used criticism, anger, shame and blame when students didn't follow the rules, I suspect that most parents would be horrified and refuse to allow their children to remain in such an environment. And so it goes in families. Staying stuck in negativity is unhealthy and unacceptable.

Terrific Tools

The goal of the Cooperation Counts system is not to have perfectly well-behaved kids. That would be great, but highly unlikely. A realistic goal is to offer simple tools that can be used in easy as well as tough times.

Compassionate parenting is a must, especially when children are misbehaving.

Raising emotionally healthy children depends on the adults in their lives—all of the adults. The emotional health of the family is vital. Finding ways to face this challenge is essential.

CHAPTER 10
PORTABLE 3'S AND STARS

SHARING 3'S

The emotional health of the family is the big picture. Each parenting scene that is handled respectfully contributes to that all important goal. Of course, there is the matter of helping kids and teens to take responsibility for their own decisions, but helping them to do so in ways that applaud the positive choices, address the poor ones, and then move on, are the most effective paths. Letting go of the anger part of parenting is a big challenge, but it is do-able. For example, how about the idea of sharing 3's as added ways to get those work-offs done and over with? This concept fits right into the bigger goals and can come in very handy in what is usually busy daily life.

JEFF AND THE NICE, COOL POOL

If Jeff has decided to get some 3's, and since sharing is a good thing, how about sending the 3's along with him if he is going to visit someone who is willing to help out with working them off? If that person agrees, here is how it could work.

Aunt Sylvia is picking up Jeff to join the cousins for swimming at Grandma's pool. When she comes to get him, some of the 3's that he has not yet worked off are handed over to go with him. This can be done on a note or even on a sticky note—something that can easily be seen. Let's say that Jeff has six 3's at home and none have been worked off yet. It could be quite easy to get one, some, or even all of them worked off with Aunt Sylvia's help—only, of course, if she agrees and would be a reliable work-off person.

Let's say the kids are all getting into the pool. Of course, it needs to be ascertained that Jeff really wants to get into the pool (this will not be an acceptable work-off if, for example, the water is too cold and Jeff is not that keen on getting into it). But let's say that Jeff is ready to jump into the (perfect temperature) pool where the other kids are already having a great time.

Oops! **"Jeff, I've checked your chart (sticky note). I see one 3. No shower on Tuesday night. The work-off is losing ten minutes of pool time. The time starts when you are all settled down."** If Jeff decides to cooperate with that, great. End of story, beginning of swimming!

If, instead, Jeff decides to be rude, talk back, or put a toe in the water, Aunt Sylvia can say (empathetically, in an adult tone of voice and with very few words) **"Oh dear. The time needs**

to start all over." Aunt Sylvia should cheer him on during the work-off: **"Only six more minutes to go. Great!"**

If Jeff decides to have any trouble during the work-off, Aunt Sylvia might decide to give counting clues about tone of voice, unkind words, etc., and if Jeff is motivated enough to get into the pool, this is his chance to get the work-off done and head for the water. The choice is completely up to him, and if this were to be so, Aunt Sylvia would, of course, be thrilled! The amount of time with a work-off like this is often not important. What is important is that it has happened at all. At the end of the day, Jeff will come home with all or some of the original 3's worked off and with not one lecture in sight.

Of course, Jeff could also come home with additional stars!

CONNECTING HOME AND SCHOOL WITH 3'S AND STARS

Sometimes it happens that kids think that when they leave their front door and enter the front door of school, there is no connection between the two locations. This is one of those situations when a lot of talk is just that—a lot of talk—and getting kids' attention is not easy. Cooperation Counts tools can easily, much to everyone's surprise, address this gray area. Teachers usually can't change their routines, and it's not fair to ask them to accommodate one student when there are lots of others needing help. If teachers agree to use the Cooperation Counts system, that's fine. If not, that's fine, too, but if they are willing, here's how they can help:

Have Cooperation Counts in place at home so that the kids already get the idea.

Ask the teacher if there are behaviors of concern, as well as positive ones.

Parents can translate that information (notes, conversations, emails, phone) into 3's and stars and add them to the home charts. School 3's will get worked off, while school stars are applauded. Note: there may be consequences and awards in place at school, which, of course, will stay. Usually, there are many more consequences as well as star opportunities at home than there are at school, where options are often limited.

Sometimes, school 3's and stars are noted in a different color on the home charts so that they can easily be identified.

As always, the kids have the power to cooperate or not. Home and school are now officially connected. The kids decide to cooperate or not, to get stars or 3's. It's up to them. As a nice addition to using this system of tracking school information, patterns of concern and strengths are more easily identified, and finding solutions can be less complicated.

CHAPTER 11

COOL COMMENTS

KIDS' CORNER

From Fran (age four)

One afternoon, Fran and her mom came upon a surprising scene in the supermarket. An angry mother was pulling her little boy's hair! While being navigated away as quickly as possible, Fran put her hand out towards the yelling mother and said, "STOP! 1,2,3!" Soon, they slowed to a more comfortable cart pace and Fran said, "That mom was too mad. I wanted to say "That's one" to her." Out of the mouths of babes!

From Ellie (age six)

"I have a big wish. I want to get three stars today. That would make me the happiest girl. I just know I can do it!" Not only did she meet her goal of three stars, she earned many more, but there was someone else who was in the really happy category— it was her Mom.

From Bill (age nine)

Bill was trying really hard to wiggle out of a work-off (which, of course, is an impossibility) and came up with the following: "Mom, I don't think you quite have the concept of the 3's yet." This was said quite seriously. Valiant try, Bill.

From Rosie (age nine)

In Rosie's family, work-offs had usually involved some sort of delay, waiting and losing time from something important. Much to her mother's surprise, one day Rosie began singing the following: "3's are yukky, stars are great. If you get a 3 you have to wait." This child might find herself with a recording contract on her hands.

From Candice (age ten)

Candice (an ADHD cooperator), whose family had mastered the Cooperation Counts program, told me: "You know, I'm going to tell my friend and her mother about this. They should be doing it, because I have the hardest time when I go out with them. They're always fighting with each other. I don't like it and I don't think they do either. If they would do more cooperating, then we could have more fun. Yes, I think I will tell them about it."

From Dan (age fourteen)

When his Dad raised his voice, Dan shared the following: "You're not doing it right. You're supposed to use a calm voice and give information, not yell at me!" I encouraged Dad to respond by saying—calmly if at all possible—**"Thank you for letting me know."** No lectures.

PARENTS' CORNER

A Divorced Dad Writes:

"The Hamburg methods have certainly reduced the previously-in-place chaos! Many parenting strategies are presented in such complicated theoretical terms that it is hard to even get started with them. Then there is the Cooperation Counts program. No matter what level of education or experience one has, Cooperation Counts can be easily understood and begun immediately. Don't be fooled; there is a vast amount of theory behind the easy steps but they are easy to learn, and the adults and the kids can jump right in!

Jean's program cuts through the complications of what to do when the kids are deciding not to cooperate. Even a child with developmental challenges can understand Cooperation Counts.

It is clear what to expect and that is very important. Having the charts detaches the adults from the conflicts part of parenting. Decisions can be made in matter-of-fact ways rather than on an emotional track. Before Cooperation Counts, our child fed off of our emotions. No more. Cooperation Counts gives us an order and a structure. It is a little like a release valve for the pressure cooker of adult emotions."

Getting Away from Giving In: A Mom Sharing Her Parents' House Writes:

"The thing with me is that I didn't do what I said and my kids knew it. I tried and tried and it was always the same. I was a wreck. They are great kids, but they were always arguing with me. I went to work and I was exhausted before I began the day, and I worried about them all the time. We live with my parents and they shouldn't have had to live with this stuff either. All they wanted to do is help us, but my kids were loud and wouldn't listen. I know it's my fault but I couldn't help it.

As soon as we started using Cooperation Counts, the boys tested and tested. In just a few days, the kids had accumulated quite a lot of 3's. I wanted to get them worked off as quickly as possible, so I took them all to the video store. I had a plan. I was shocked at myself. I was calm. I knew just what to do. We found a game that we had all been wanting for a long time. Everyone was so excited. I just waited. When we got up to the clerk to pay for it, I acted shocked—and said that I had almost forgotten but they each had four 3's and the work-off of all of them was no video game that night. They went mental. They were screaming and hollering, telling me to shut up.... I was calm, told them that work-offs of those nasty 3's was really sad. We left the store with them screaming and hollering all the way home but we left the video store without the video game. I said nothing more.

The next day I would say there was about fifty percent more co-operation, which was a big improvement, and my parents, who hadn't wanted to have anything to do with this system, saw that things were settling down. This morning, my oldest son had a problem with his sneakers and ended up talking with his grand-father. He said that his sneakers were old, they were dirty, and that he couldn't possibly wear them. My father told him that there wasn't enough money for new sneakers and that the most important thing was that they still fit him. He said that part of growing up was waiting for things.

My son came to me a few minutes later and told me that he was thinking that this might be the day he was starting to grow up. He was going to wait for his sneakers. I couldn't believe it.

When there are troubles—and there are lots of them—I know what to do now, and the kids know that there will be work-off's if they make poor choices, and there will be stars and smiling if they make positive ones. I can't believe how different I feel as a person and as a parent."

Comment: This was a brave Mom and she did just the right thing. She waited until there was an appropriate work-off that was re-ally important to the kids. Knowing what to do vs. not having a clue gave her confidence. There was a plan. She was able to speak in a respectful tone. She was willing to wait through the wailing due to the lack of a video game that day. Getting the kids' attention and following through with discipline and praise helped the entire family—including the grandparents!

A Mother of One Writes:

"The value of this program goes beyond what it has done for my daughter. To me, one of the most priceless and crucial changes has been in my own behavior, attitude, and psyche. Prior to beginning our work with the program, there was endless negativity in our home. The Cooperation Counts program taught me alternative methods that could handle every potential situation that might arise with our daughter. I feel like an elephant has been lifted from my back. I've learned techniques and new ways of thinking that have changed my life forever, and through my own changes, that is what has helped my child. The Cooperation Counts program makes perfect sense and is easy to use each and every day."

A Mother of Two Writes:

"One of the most helpful parts of the Cooperation Counts program was giving me ways to stop nagging and lecturing my kids. Like most parents, I assumed that it was my job to teach them the right ways to do things. I wasn't wrong, but my methods were. I discovered that I was using the *same* lecture template for almost any given topic—the "late for school" , "do your homework" .or the "get ready for bed" lectures. Using the time warnings, counting clues, working off of 3's , stars, and 'use only a very few words' rules are so much more effective!

For example, my child does not want to go to bed because she wants to see a TV program. Cooperation Counts has taught me that it is not about me, it is not even a defiance of me. She just wants to watch TV. But, oops, it's bedtime. So the TV goes off. Before we used the system, I knew intellectually that I shouldn't be taking things personally. Now, I know it for real.

By using the program, I see that lectures and nagging just escalated the entire situation and provided the music and the lyrics for high drama. It got to the point where I wasn't even listening to my own lectures. No wonder the kids tuned me out.

At first, when Cooperation Counts came into our home and the lecturing stopped, the silence was really strange. It was as if each of us was waiting for the show to start. The few words and no nagging tools are much more comfortable for us now, and we are even having real conversations!

The best thing about using the stars, aside from the fact that I love giving them and the kids love getting them, is that they can't be touched. Even if a difficult behavior follows, stars stay.

Now, I'm on the look-out for star efforts. I love the surprised look on their faces when I notice something kind they've done, or the use of self-control or something smart or insightful that

I might never have noticed before. It's more genuine than just general praise, more personal. Now, the kids get filled up with all of the kind and helpful and cooperative things I notice they do. It's the little things, after all, that really make or break a family. Now, when my daughter remembers to put the cap on the toothpaste, believe me I notice and she's deciding to do it a whole lot more of the time.

Looking out for stars also reminds me how great my kids truly are. It's so hard, sometimes, to reach beyond the behavior or even a diagnosis to see the child inside. Sometimes, when I'm particularly exasperated—I look at their star charts. Doing this reminds me of who they really are and how hard they try, at least some of the time. Of course, we look at their star charts together, too, but when I want to get beyond frustrating moments, taking a peek just by myself helps to ground me.

Each of my girls has different emotional challenges. Something that might be easy positive behavior for my organizationally-obsessed older daughter (getting her homework bag ready without even being asked, etc) is a really hard behavior to master for my younger one. If she even manages to remember she *has* a homework bag and puts it by the door, that's a star for her!

Working off the 3's was the hardest part for me because of the fear that outbursts would happen, escalate, and become out of control. However, the need to make the work-offs happen (since that is my job), has caused me to examine my own inner fears. I have learned how to tailor the work-offs to my children's individualized needs and to my own threshold of fear. Slowly,

I became expert in making them more meaningful. They never became harsh, but they got to have a little more "directional muscle" behind them. Now I understand that it is not as important *what* the work-off is but *that it has happened at all.*

The idea of the work-off is probably more effective than the actual work-off itself, and it became easier as I came to fear my children's reactions less.

Perhaps one of the best things about the way work-offs happen is that they gave me the space between the action and the consequence. Sometimes, I have to admit, when my kids enraged me, I wanted revenge and to wield parental power. "You're going to throw a tantrum in the car, fine..... no ice-cream at Dairy Queen." It is a kind of parental revenge that might have feel good for a split second, but it is truly not productive. It only serves to model revenge-like behavior to my kids. I took away the ice-cream and they started to kick the back of my car seat. No one wins in that situation.

The sequence of time warnings, counting clues, work-offs, and stars changed everything. Following through with a well-thought-out consequence does not come out as parental revenge, as does the immediate imposition of a punishment.

Using the Cooperation Counts steps changes everything. With the way work-offs are done, the power was in the kids' hands to start with. I was initially worried that the time distance between the problem and the work-off would cause my kids to forget the "why" of the consequence. That really doesn't seem to be the case. The problem is written in a visible place. We use the regular 3's charts. Waiting for work-offs defuses the anger of the high-drama moment, and they become what they are—a consequence for a behavior that wasn't the most helpful or cooperative choice. There can be, of course, those 3's that have an immediate and very directly related consequence. The program has lots of flexibility, which is good.

Let's face it. When the adult is on task, the whole family runs better, and using the system has been a literal lifesaver. Now, if I get off track, the kids remind me to use warnings and counting clues so that yelling and lecturing stops.

Thank goodness the steps are simple because being a parent certainly is not!"

A Father of Three Writes:

"Cooperation Counts is clear, effective, and powerful. What has happened is that I am not the bad guy anymore. We have discipline in our house now but we also have a lot of fun.

Because I resent my kids less, I can love them more."

A Mom With Four Kids Writes:

"It was really hard to start. I never thought I could follow through. I thought the kids would be so mad at me and it would only be worse. But I counted and I waited and I finally figured out what to do. My oldest (who has multiple medications and is in a behavior-based classroom) began karate lessons. I saw how much he loved it. I took him to several lessons.....and I waited....until one day, before his karate lesson, I called up the teacher and asked if it would be OK to bring him, but only to let him watch, because he was working off a 3. He agreed. We parked, walked up to the studio, opened the front door—and then I said, in a sad voice, that I had checked his chart, and saw a bunch of 3's. Two of them would be worked off by watching the lesson—not participating. I told him, empathetically, that the teacher knew about the just-watching plan and had agreed. My son looked like he couldn't believe this, but that's what we did. He watched, and when we got home, he talked to his brothers and sister and he must have told them something about what had happened, because the house has been nice and quiet. Amazing."

Note the "Ripple Effect": The other kids decided to save themselves from 3's. Now that's interesting: A work-off for one child turned into more cooperation by four!

This simple method of behavior management gives parents concrete daily life tools to address normal, usual, age-appropriate difficulties as well as more intense, disruptive ones.

CHAPTER 12

COMPLACENCY: READY FOR THE WRINKLES

So there you are! You have set up a system of discipline and praise that is applicable to virtually every difficult family situation, one that works within a very short time and that leaves your dignity and your children's dignity intact. But as I write this book, families are reminding me to include something about the dangers of complacency.

This can happen when the household is more peaceful, when there are fewer times of trouble, or even when troubled times continue to a lesser degree. When handled in the Cooperation Counts way, trouble will appear less dramatic. The adults know what to do. The kids know what to do. Stress is minimized. Counting clues are needed less frequently, and there are stretches of time when there are not even any 3's charts in sight. Compliments have continued and things have gone along pretty well.

Then "it" happens. Trouble arrives once again. Someone is acting up, or there may be a real crisis or even a family emergency.

These are the times I tend to get calls from back-to-being-frantic parents. Since relationships and daily life are full of complicated dynamics and emotions, it's natural to assume that the sensitive balance of relationships will encounter rough seas, either predictably or unexpectedly.

In the discipline and praise departments, it's back-to-basics time.

Cooperation Counts strategies can be implemented during the storms of difficulties as well as the times of smooth sailing. Often, the initial panic call from Cooperation Counts parents of "Help, trouble!" is followed by another, like "I figured it out. It was me. I was yelling and being critical again." This sort of self-reflection is wonderful and helps with heading back to treating each other respectfully, giving everyone the chance to be heard and understood, as well as tightening up the boundaries that must be in place for the safety and security of all.

THE SYSTEM SUMMARY
When the Adults are Serious

The Cooperation Counts program provides a framework for effective discipline with dignity along with plentiful praise for all.

1. Stay focused on one behavior at a time.

2. Use very few words.

3. Make a statement instead of asking a question.

4. Give a time warning whenever possible.

5. Begin counting clues as described in Chapter 1.

6. Follow the work-off steps as described in Chapter 2.

Always Watch for the Stars!

Give stars for star choices as described in Chapter 3.

Use the system to: find ways to remain calm in challenging moments and avoid power struggles that inevitably lead to no good. As we are able to get the kids' attention in respectful, clear ways, it is then that there can be thoughtful rather than impulsive parenting and we can move on to the pleasures of family life!

Keep Your CC Life Preserver at the Ready!

Parenting is never an easy ride. Under the best of circumstances, we will experience incredible joys and gut-wrenching lows, as well as every emotion in between. Just when we think there is smooth sailing, storms pop up, often without any warning!

Parenting involves not only discipline and praise. Everything having to do with important relationships involves waves of unpredictability.

Having parenting strategies that can be used easily, in everyday life as well as in a crisis, is like using the proverbial life preserver at just the right time to avoid being swept out to sea.

It is always wise to employ the user-friendly guidelines of the Cooperation Counts program, while navigating the challenging course of relationships with our children and each other. So, hold on tight and enjoy the complicated but wonderful world of parenting.

AFTERWORD:
PEACE ON EARTH

When there is cooperation, there is a better chance that family values can be shared in calmer, more positive ways.

When family values can be shared in calmer ways, there is a better chance for kids and adults to try their best.

When kids and adults try their best, they can grow together in happier ways.

When kids and adults are happier, there is less anger.

When there is less anger, there is more room for love.

When there is more love, there is less violence.

When there is less violence, there is less hate.

When there is less hate, there is a chance for more thoughtful, positive choices .

When there are more thoughtful, positive choices, there is a chance for more kindness and peace within families.

When there is more kindness and peace within families, there is more of a chance for kindness and peace in our communities.

If there is more cooperation, kindness, and peace in our communities, there is a chance for kindness and peace in many communities when children move into adulthood.

If there are more peaceful adults and kids with healthy, positive values, there would be more of a chance for peace in our world community.

I have never been aware of a war situation where cooperation, compromise, and kindness were ingredients.

One might hope that the impact of more peaceful families could help to replace at least some hostility, prejudice, and hate in our shared world community and help with the search for ultimate peace on earth.

Cooperation Certainly Does Count!

A Final Note to my Readers

Parenting is a personal journey with surprises at every turn. As there is a universal longing to foster positive connections with our children, it is my hope that this book will help to do just that.

Jean Hamburg

CPSIA information can be obtained at www.ICGtesting.com
Printed in the USA
BVOW031343021111

275103BV00001B/147/P